From a photograph by C. R. Eagle.

Atlantic Fleet steaming in line of bearing.

OUR NAVY IN THE WAR

AMERICA IN THE WAR

OUR NAVY IN THE WAR

BY

LAWRENCE PERRY

Ross & Perry, Inc.
Washington, D.C.

© Ross & Perry, Inc. 2001 All rights reserved.

Protected under the Berne Convention. Published 2001

Printed in The United States of America
Ross & Perry, Inc. Publishers
717 Second St., N.E., Suite 200
Washington, D.C. 20002
Telephone (202) 675-8300
Facsimile (801) 459-7535
info@RossPerry.com

SAN 253-8555

Library of Congress Control Number: 2001097012
http://www.rossperry.com

ISBN 1-931839-12-3

Image on Cover provided by www.history.navy.mil

☮ The paper used in this publication meets the requirements for permanence established by the American National Standard for Information Sciences "Permanence of Paper for Printed Library Materials" (ANSI Z39.48-1984).

All rights reserved. No copyrighted part of this publication may be reproduced, stored in a retrieval system, or transmitted, in any form or by any means, electronic, photocopying, recording, or otherwise, without the prior written permission of the publisher.

THIS BOOK

IS RESPECTFULLY DEDICATED TO THE

HON. JOSEPHUS DANIELS

A NEWSPAPER MAN WHO BROUGHT TO HIS TASK AS SECRETARY OF THE NAVY THOSE GREAT QUALITIES OF MIND AND CHARACTER WHICH FITTED HIM TO MEET WITH SUCH SIGNAL SUCCESS THE IMMENSE PROBLEMS WHICH THE WAR IMPOSED UPON HIS OFFICE. TO HIS FAR-SEEING VISION, HIS BREADTH OF VIEW, HIS FREEDOM FROM ALL BIAS, HIS JUDGMENT OF MEN AND OF AFFAIRS, AND TO THE STERN COURAGE OF HIS CONVICTIONS ARE DUE TO-DAY THE MAINTENANCE OF THOSE HIGH TRADITIONS OF THE UNITED STATES NAVY OF WHICH AMERICANS HAVE EVER BEEN PROUD

CONTENTS

FOREWORD 1

CHAPTER I

FIRST EXPERIENCE OF OUR NAVY WITH THE GERMAN U-BOAT—ARRIVAL OF CAPTAIN HANS ROSE AND THE U-53 AT NEWPORT—EXPERIENCES OF THE GERMAN SAILORS IN AN AMERICAN PORT—DESTRUCTION OF MERCHANTMAN BY U-53 OFF NANTUCKET—OUR DESTROYERS TO THE RESCUE—SCENES IN NEWPORT—GERMAN REJOICING—THE NAVY PREPARES FOR WAR 26

CHAPTER II

OUR NAVY ARMS AMERICAN MERCHANT VESSELS—DEATH OF OUR FIRST BLUEJACKET ON SERVICE IN THE WAR ZONE—VICE-ADMIRAL SIMS—WE TAKE OVER PATROL OF WATERS OF WESTERN HEMISPHERE—THE NAVAL ADVISORY BOARD OF INVENTIONS—WORK OF THIS BODY—OUR BATTLESHIPS THE LARGEST IN THE WORLD—WIDESPREAD OPERATIONS 42

CHAPTER III

FIRST HOSTILE CONTACT BETWEEN THE NAVY AND THE GERMANS—ARMED GUARDS ON MERCHANT VESSELS—"CAMPANA" FIRST TO SAIL—DANIELS REFUSES OFFER OF MONEY AWARDS TO MEN WHO SINK SUBMARINES—"MONGOLIA" SHOWS GERMANY HOW THE YANKEE SAILORMAN BITES—FIGHT OF THE "SILVERSHELL"—HEROISM OF GUNNERS ON MERCHANT SHIPS—SINKING OF THE "ANTILLES"—EXPERIENCES OF VOYAGERS 59

CONTENTS

CHAPTER IV

PAGE

DESTROYERS ON GUARD—PREPARATIONS OF FLOTILLA TO CROSS THE OCEAN—MEETING THE "ADRIATIC"—FLOTILLA ARRIVES IN QUEENSTOWN—RECEPTION BY BRITISH COMMANDER AND POPULACE—"WE ARE READY NOW, SIR"—ARRIVAL OF THE FAMOUS CAPTAIN EVANS ON THE AMERICAN FLAG-SHIP—OUR NAVY A WARM-WEATHER NAVY—LOSS OF THE "VACUUM" 79

CHAPTER V

BRITISH AND AMERICAN DESTROYERS OPERATING HAND IN HAND—ARRIVAL OF NAVAL COLLIER "JUPITER"—SUCCESSFUL TRIP OF TRANSPORTS BEARING UNITED STATES SOLDIERS CONVOYED BY NAVAL VESSELS—ATTACK ON TRANSPORTS WARDED OFF BY DESTROYERS—SECRETARY BAKER THANKS SECRETARY DANIELS—VISIT TO OUR DESTROYER BASE—ATTITUDE OF OFFICERS TOWARD MEN—GENESIS OF THE SUBMARINE—THE CONFEDERATE SUBMARINE "HUNLEY" 96

CHAPTER VI

ON A GERMAN SUBMARINE—FIGHT WITH A DESTROYER—PERISCOPE HIT—RECORD OF THE SUBMARINE IN THIS WAR—DAWNING FAILURE OF THE UNDERSEA BOAT—FIGURES ISSUED BY THE BRITISH ADMIRALTY—PROOF OF DECLINE—OUR NAVY'S PART IN THIS ACHIEVEMENT . 117

CHAPTER VII

HOW THE SUBMARINE IS BEING FOUGHT—DESTROYERS THE GREAT MENACE—BUT NETS, TOO, HAVE PLAYED THEIR PART—MANY OTHER DEVICES—GERMAN OFFICERS TELL OF EXPERIENCE ON A SUBMARINE CAUGHT IN A NET—CHASERS PLAY THEIR PART—THE DEPTH-BOMB—TRAWLER TRICKS—A CAMOUFLAGED SCHOONER WHICH TURNED OUT TO BE A TARTAR—AIRPLANES—GERMAN SUBMARINE MEN IN PLAYFUL MOOD 135

CONTENTS

CHAPTER VIII

PERILS AND TRIUMPHS OF SUBMARINE-HUNTING—THE LOSS OF OUR FIRST WAR-SHIP, THE CONVERTED GUNBOAT "ALCEDO"—BRAVERY OF CREW—"CASSIN" STRUCK BY TORPEDO BUT REMAINS IN THE FIGHT—LOSS OF THE "JACOB JONES"—SINKING OF THE "SAN DIEGO"—DESTROYERS "NICHOLSON" AND "FANNING" CAPTURE A SUBMARINE WHICH SINKS—CREW OF GERMANS BROUGHT INTO PORT—THE POLICY OF SILENCE IN REGARD TO SUBMARINE SINKINGS 156

CHAPTER IX

OUR BATTLESHIP FLEET—GREAT WORKSHOP OF WAR—PREPARATIONS FOR FOREIGN SERVICE—ON A BATTLESHIP DURING A SUBMARINE ATTACK—THE WIRELESS THAT WENT WRONG—THE TORPEDO THAT MISSED—ATTACK ON SUBMARINE BASES OF DOUBTFUL EXPEDIENCY—WHEN THE GERMAN FLEET COMES OUT—ESTABLISHMENT OF STATION IN THE AZORES 181

CHAPTER X

THE GREAT ATLANTIC FERRY COMPANY, INCORPORATED, BUT UNLIMITED—FEAT OF THE NAVY IN REPAIRING THE STEAMSHIPS BELONGING TO GERMAN LINES WHICH WERE INTERNED AT BEGINNING OF WAR IN 1914—WELDING AND PATCHING—TRIUMPH OF OUR NAVY WITH THE "VATERLAND"—HER CONDITION—KNOTS ADDED TO HER SPEED—DAMAGE TO MOTIVE POWER AND HOW IT WAS REMEDIED—FAMOUS GERMAN LINERS BROUGHT UNDER OUR FLAG 198

CHAPTER XI

CAMOUFLAGE—AMERICAN SYSTEM OF LOW VISIBILITY AND THE BRITISH DAZZLE SYSTEM—AMERICANS WORKED OUT PRINCIPLES OF COLOR IN LIGHT AND COLOR IN PIGMENT—BRITISH SOUGHT MERELY TO CONFUSE THE EYE—BRITISH SYSTEM APPLIED TO SOME OF OUR TRANSPORTS 217

CONTENTS

CHAPTER XII

PAGE

THE NAVAL FLYING CORPS—WHAT THE NAVY DEPARTMENT HAS ACCOMPLISHED AND IS ACCOMPLISHING IN THE WAY OF AIR-FIGHTING—EXPERIENCE OF A NAVAL ENSIGN ADRIFT IN THE ENGLISH CHANNEL—SEAPLANES AND FLYING BOATS—SCHOOLS OF INSTRUCTION—INSTANCES OF HEROISM 224

CHAPTER XIII

ORGANIZATION OF THE NAVAL RESERVE CLASSES—TAKING OVER OF YACHTS FOR NAVAL SERVICE—WORK AMONG THE RESERVES STATIONED AT VARIOUS NAVAL CENTRES —WALTER CAMP'S ACHIEVEMENT 239

CHAPTER XIV

THE UNITED STATES MARINE CORPS—FIRST MILITARY BRANCH OF THE NATIONAL SERVICE TO BE SANCTIONED BY CONGRESS—LEAVING FOR THE WAR—SERVICE OF THE MARINES IN VARIOUS PARTS OF THE GLOBE—DETAILS OF EXPANSION OF CORPS—THEIR PRESENT SERVICE ALL OVER THE WORLD 260

CHAPTER XV

SCOPE OF THE NAVY'S WORK IN VARIOUS PARTICULARS— FOOD—FUEL—NAVAL CONSULTING BOARD—PROJECTILE FACTORY—EXPENDITURES—INCREASE OF PERSONNEL 272

CHAPTER XVI

THE BEGINNING OF THE END—REPORTS IN LONDON THAT SUBMARINES WERE WITHDRAWING TO THEIR BASES TO HEAD A BATTLE MOVEMENT ON THE PART OF THE GERMAN FLEET—HOW THE PLAN WAS FOILED—THE SURRENDER OF THE GERMAN FLEET TO THE COMBINED BRITISH AND AMERICAN SQUADRONS—DEPARTURE OF THE AMERICAN SQUADRON—WHAT MIGHT HAVE HAPPENED HAD THE GERMAN VESSELS COME OUT TO FIGHT 280

CONTENTS

CHAPTER XVII

LESSONS OF THE WAR—THE SUBMARINE NOT REALLY A SUBMARINE—FRENCH TERM FOR UNDERSEA FIGHTER—THE SUCCESS OF THE CONVOY AGAINST SUBMERSIBLES—U-BOATS NOT SUCCESSFUL AGAINST SURFACE FIGHTERS—THEIR SHORTCOMINGS—WHAT THE SUBMARINE NEEDS TO BE A VITAL FACTOR IN SEA POWER—THEIR SHOWING AGAINST CONVOYED CRAFT—RECORD OF OUR NAVY IN CONVOYING AND PROTECTING CONVOYS 294

SECRETARY DANIELS'S REPORT 307

ILLUSTRATIONS

Atlantic Fleet steaming in line of bearing . . . . *Frontispiece*

FACING PAGE

Portraits of Josephus Daniels, Secretary of the Navy, Rear-Admiral Leigh C. Palmer, Vice-Admiral William S. Sims, Admiral Henry T. Mayo, Rear-Admiral Albert Gleaves, Admiral William S. Benson 22

Position of ships in a convoy 100

A U. S. submarine at full speed on the surface of the water 130

A submarine-chaser 146

A torpedo-destroyer 146

Repairing a damaged cylinder of a German ship for federal service 208

Scene at an aviation station somewhere in America, showing fifteen seaplanes on beach departing and arriving 234

Captain's inspection at Naval Training Station, Newport, R. I. 246

American Marines who took part in the Marne offensive on parade in Paris, July 4, 1918 268

OUR NAVY IN THE WAR

FOREWORD

GENTLY rolling and heaving on the surge of a summer sea lay a mighty fleet of war-vessels. There were the capital ships of the Atlantic Fleet, grim dreadnoughts with their superimposed turrets, their bristling broadsides, their basket-masts—veritable islands of steel. There were colliers, hospital-ships, destroyers, patrol-vessels—in all, a tremendous demonstration of our sea power. Launches were dashing hither and thither across the restless blue waters, signal-flags were flashing from mast and stay and the wind, catching the sepia reek from many a funnel, whipped it across a league of sea.

On the deck of the largest battleship were gathered the officers of the fleet not only, but nearly every officer on active duty in home waters. All eyes were turned shoreward and presently as a sharp succession of shots rang out a sleek, narrow craft with gracefully turned bow came out from the horizon and advanced swiftly toward the flag-ship. It was the President's yacht, the *Mayflower*, with the President of the United States on board. As the yacht swung to a launch was dropped overside, the gangway lowered and Woodrow Wilson stepped down to the little craft, bobbing on the waves. There was no salute, no pomp, no official circumstance, nor anything in the way of ceremony. The President did not want that.

What he did want was to meet the officers of our navy and give them a heart-to-heart talk. He did just that. At the time it was early summer in 1917. In the preceding April a declaration that Germany had been waging war upon the United States had been made in Congress; war resolutions had been passed and signed by the President. This on April 6. On April 7 the Navy Department had put into effect plans that had already been formulated. Much had been done when the President boarded the flag-ship of the Atlantic Fleet that early summer afternoon. Some of our destroyers

FOREWORD

were already at work in foreign waters, but the bulk of our fighting force was at home, preparing for conflict. And it was this time that the President chose to meet those upon whom the nation relied to check the submarine and to protect our shores against the evil devices of the enemy.

"He went," wrote a narrator of this historic function, "directly to the business in hand. And the business in hand was telling the officers of the navy of the United States that the submarine had to be beaten and that they had to do it. He talked—well, it must still remain a secret, but if you have ever heard a football coach talk to his team between the halves; if you ever heard a captain tell his men what he expected of them as they stripped for action; if you ever knew what the fighting spirit of Woodrow Wilson really is when it is on fire— then you can visualize the whole scene. He wanted not merely as good a record from our navy as other navies had, he wanted a better record. He wanted action, not merely from the gold-braided admirals, but from the ensigns, too; and he wanted every mind turned to the solution of the submarine question, and regardless of rank and distinction he wanted all to work and fight for the common object—victory.

"Somebody suggested to the President later that the speech be published. He declined. Most of it wasn't said to be published. It was a direct talk from the commander-in-chief of the navy to his men. It was inspiration itself. The officers cheered and went away across the seas. And there they have been in action ever since, giving an account of themselves that has already won the admiration of their allies and the involuntary respect of their foes."

It was under such auspices as these that the United States Navy went forth to war. No one ever doubted the spirit of our fighters of the sea. Through all the years, from the time when John Paul Jones bearded enemy ships in their own waters, when *Old Ironsides* belched forth her well-directed broadsides in many a victorious encounter; when Decatur showed the pirates of Tripoli that they had a new power with which to deal; when Farragut damned the torpedoes in Mobile Bay, and Dewey did

FOREWORD

likewise in Manila Bay; when Sampson and Schley triumphed at Santiago, and Hobson accepted the seemingly fatal chance under the guns of Morro Castle—through all the years, I say, and through all that they have brought in the way of armed strife, the nation never for one moment has ever doubted the United States Navy.

And neither did Woodrow Wilson doubt. He knew his men. But he wanted to look them all in the eye and tell them that he knew their mettle, knew what they could do, and held no thought of their failure. Every fighting man fights the better for an incident of this sort.

Week by week since that time there has come to us from out the grim North Sea, from the Mediterranean and the broad Atlantic abundant testimony, many a story of individual and collective heroism, of ships that have waged gallant fights, of Americans who have lived gallantly, who have died gloriously—and above all there has come to us the gratifying record of reduced submarine losses, as to which there is abundant testimony—notably from the great maritime and naval power of the world—Great Britain—that our navy has played a vital part in the diminution of the undersea terror.

Less than a year after President Wilson boarded the flag-ship of the Atlantic Fleet our navy had more than 150 naval vessels—battleships, cruisers, submarines and tenders, gunboats, coast-guard cutters, converted yachts, tugs, and numerous vessels of other types for special purposes—in European waters. Serving on these vessels were nearly 40,000 men, more than half the strength of our navy before we entered the war—and this number did not include the personnel of troop-ships, supply-vessels, armed guards for merchantmen, signalmen, wireless operators and the like, who go into the war zone on recurrent trips.

Submarines have been fought and sunk or captured—how many, a wise naval policy bids absolute silence. Our antisubmarine activities now cover in war areas alone over 1,000,000 square miles of sea. In a six-months period one detachment of destroyers steamed over 1,000,000 of miles in the war zone, attacked 81 submarines, escorted 717 single vessels, participated in 86 convoys, and spent one hundred and fifty days at sea.

There have been mistakes, of course; there have been delays which have tried the patience not only of the country, but of the Navy Department. But they were inevitable under the high pressure of affairs as they suddenly set in when we went to war. But in looking back over the year and a half of conflict, considering the hundreds of thousands of soldiers that our navy has conducted in safety across the infested Atlantic, and the feats which our fighters have performed in action, in stormy seas, in rescue work and in the long, weary grind of daily routine, no American has cause for aught but pride in the work our navy has done.

There has been more than a sixfold increase in naval man power and about a fourfold increase in the number of ships in service. When present plans have been carried out—and all projects are proceeding swiftly—the United States will probably rank second to Britain among naval Powers of the world. Training facilities have increased on a stupendous scale;

we have now various specialized schools for seamen and officers; our industrial yards have grown beyond dreams and the production of ordnance and munitions proceeds on a vast scale, while in other directions things have been accomplished by the Navy Department which will not be known until the war is over and the records are open for all to read.

But in the meantime history has been making and facts have been marked which give every American pride. Praise from the source of all things maritime is praise indeed, and what greater commendation—better than anything that might be spoken or written—could be desired than the action of Admiral Sir David Beatty, commander-in-chief of the Grand Fleet, who, receiving a report not so many months ago that the German High Seas Fleet was out, awarded the post of honor in the consolidated fleet of British and American war-vessels which went forth to meet the Germans to a division of American battleships. This chivalrous compliment on the part of the British commander was no doubt designed as a signal act of courtesy, but more, it was born of the confidence of a man who has seen our navy, who had had the most complete opportunities for studying it and, as a consequence, knew what it could do.

There is nothing of chauvinism in the statement that, so far as the submarine is concerned, our navy has played a most helpful part in diminishing its ravages, that our fighting ships have aided very materially in the marked reduction in sinkings of merchantmen as compared to the number destroyed in the corresponding period before we entered the war, and in the no less notable increase in the number of submarines captured or sunk. These facts have not only been made clear by official Navy Department statements, but have been attested to by many British and French Admiralty and Government authorities and naval commanders.

"You doubtless know," wrote Admiral Sims to the Secretary of the Navy some time ago, "that all of the Allies here with whom I am associated are very much impressed by the efforts now being made by the United States Navy Department to oppose the submarine and protect merchant shipping. I am very glad to report that our forces are more than coming up to expectations."

Admiral Sims was modest. Let us quote the message sent by Admiral Sir Lewis Bayly, commander-in-chief of the British naval forces on the Irish coast, on the anniversary of the arrival of our first destroyer flotilla at Queenstown:

"On the anniversary of the arrival of the first United States men-of-war at Queenstown I wish to express my deep gratitude to the United States officers and ratings for the skill, energy, and unfailing good nature which they all have consistently shown and which qualities have so materially assisted in the war by enabling ships of the Allied Powers to cross the ocean in comparative freedom. To command you is an honor, to work with you is a pleasure, to know you is to know the best traits of the Anglo-Saxon race."

And to Secretary Daniels, Sir Eric Geddes, first lord of the British Admiralty, wrote in part:

"As you know, we all of us here have great admiration for your officers and men and for the splendid help they are giving in European waters. Further, we find Admiral Sims invaluable in counsel and in co-operation."

American naval aid has been of the greatest help to the British Fleet, wrote Archibald Hurd, the naval expert, in the *Daily Telegraph*, London.

"When the war is over," he said, "the nation will form some conception of the extent of the debt which we owe the American Navy for the manner in which it has co-operated, not only in connection with the convoy system, but in fighting the submarines. If the naval position is improving to-day, as it is, it is due to the fact that the British and American fleets are working in closest accord, supported by an immense body of skilled workers on both sides of the Atlantic, who are turning out destroyers and other crafts for dealing with the submarines as well as mines and bombs. The Germans can have a battle whenever they want it. The strength of the Grand Fleet has been well maintained. Some of the finest battleships of the United States Navy are now associated with it. They are not only splendid fighting-ships, but they are well officered and manned."

Here is what Lord Reading, the British Ambassador to the United States said in the course of an address at the Yale 1918 Commencement:

"Let me say to you on behalf of the British people what a debt of gratitude we owe to your navy for its co-operation with us. There is no finer spectacle to be seen at present than that complete and cordial co-operation which is existing between your fleet and ours. They work as one. I always think to myself and hope that the co-operation of our fleets, of our navies, is the harbinger of what is to come in the future when the war is over, of that which will still continue then. Magnificent is their work, and I glory always in the thought that an American admiral has taken charge of the British Fleet and the British policy, and that when the plans are formed for an attack that American admiral is given the place of honor in our fleet, because we feel that it is his due at this moment."

And finally, there is the testimony of Admiral Sir Roslyn Wemyss, first sea lord of the British, concerning our effective aid, testimony, by the way, which enlightens us to some extent upon British and American methods of co-operation.

"On the broad lines of strategic policy," he said, "complete unanimity exists. Admiral Benson and Admiral Mayo have both visited us and studied our naval plans. No officers could have exhibited keener appreciation of the naval situation. I find it difficult to express the gratitude of the British service to these officers and to Admiral Sims for the support they have given us. I am not exaggerating, or camouflaging, to borrow a word of the moment. Our relations could not be more cordial. The day-to-day procedure is of the simplest. Every morning I hold conference with the principal officers of the naval staff, and Admiral Sims is present as the representative of the United States Fleet, joining freely in the discussion of the various subjects which arise. I need not add that I keenly appreciate his help. At sea the same spirit of cordial co-operation exists—extremely cordial. I should like to say we have, fortunately, a common language and common traditions, which have done much to assist us in working together.

"The American officers and men are first-rate. It is impossible to pay too high a tribute to the manner in which they settled down to this job of submarine hunting, and to the intelligence, resource, and courage which they have exhibited. They came on the scene at the opportune moment. Our men had been in the mill for many weary months. Possibly the American people, so far removed from the main theatre of the war, can hardly appreciate what it meant when these American officers and men crossed the Atlantic. They have been splendid, simply splendid. I have seen a number of the destroyers and conversed with a large number of officers. I also have had many reports and am not speaking of the aid the United States has rendered without full knowledge.

"Not only are the vessels well constructed and the officers and men thoroughly competent, but the organization is admirable. It was no slight matter for so many ships to come 3,000 miles across the Atlantic to fight in European waters. The decision raised several complicated problems in connection with supplies, but those problems have been surmounted with success. There has never been anything like it before in the history of naval warfare, and the development of the steam-engine has rendered such co-operation more difficult than ever before, because the modern man-of-war is dependent on a constant stream of supplies of fuel, stores, food, and other things, and is need of frequent repairs."

In addition to doing signally effective work in hunting down the submarine, and in protecting ocean commerce, our war-ships have relieved England and France of the necessity of looking out for raiders and submarines in South Atlantic waters; we have sent to the Grand Fleet, among other craft, a squadron of dreadnoughts and superdreadnoughts whose aggregate gun-power will tell whenever the German sea-fighters decide to risk battle in the North Sea; war-ships are convoying transports laden with thousands of men—more than a million and a half fighting men will be on French and English soil before these words are read—

escorting ocean liners and convoying merchant vessels, while in divers other ways the navy of this country is playing its dominant part in the fight against German ruthlessness.

When the Emergency Fleet Corporation announced its programme of building ships the Navy Department at once began its preparations for providing armed guards for these vessels as soon as they were commissioned for transatlantic service. Thousands of men were placed in training for this purpose and detailed instructions were prepared and issued to the Shipping Board and to all ship-building companies to enable them to prepare their vessels while building with gun-emplacements, armed-guard quarters, and the like, so that when the vessels were completed there would be as little delay as possible in furnishing them. In all details relating to the protection of these merchant vessels the navy has played a most vital part and not least of the laurels accruing to this department of the government war service for work in the present struggle have been those won by naval gun crews on cargo-laden ships.

The administrative work in connection with vessels of this class is a not inconsiderable task of itself. The romance of the armed merchantmen affords material for many a vivid page, and when in its proper place in this volume it is set forth somewhat in detail the reader will grasp—if he has not already done so through perusal of the daily press—the fact that all the glory of naval service in this war has not resided within the turrets of the dreadnought nor on the deck of destroyer or patrol-vessel.

The navy organized and has operated the large transport service required to take our soldiers overseas. At this writing not a single transport has been lost on the way to France, and but three have been sunk returning. Transports bound for France have been attacked by submarines time and again, and, in fact, our first transport convoy was unsuccessfully assailed, as has been the case with other convoys throughout the past twelve months. In the case of the *Tuscania*, sunk by a torpedo while eastbound with American soldiers, that vessel was under British convoy, a fact which implies no discredit upon the British Navy, since it is beyond the powers of human ingenuity so to protect the ocean lanes as to warrant assurance that a vessel, however well convoyed, shall be totally immune from the lurking submarine. . Again, it should be remembered, that the British have taken about sixty per cent of our expeditionary forces across the ocean.

In the line of expanding ship-building facilities the Navy Department has in the past year carried on vigorously a stupendous policy of increased shipyard capacity, which upon completion will see this country able to have in course of construction on the ways at one time sixteen war-vessels of which seven will be battleships.

In January, 1917, three months before we went to war, the Navy Department's facilities for ship-building were: Boston, one auxiliary vessel; New York, one battleship; Philadelphia, one auxiliary; Norfolk, one destroyer; Charleston, one gunboat; Mare Island, one battleship and one destroyer. At the present time the Brooklyn Navy Yard has a way for the building of dreadnoughts, and one for the building of battleships. At Philadelphia two

FOREWORD

ways are being built for large battleships and battle-cruisers. Norfolk, in addition to her one way for destroyers, will soon have a way for battleships. Charleston will have five ways for destroyers. The navy-yard at Puget Sound will soon have a way for one battleship.

The building plans include not only the construction of ways, but also machine, electrical, structural, forge, and pattern shops in addition to foundries, storehouses, railroad-tracks, and power-plants. This increase in building capacity will enable the government through enhanced repair facilities to handle all repair and building work for the fleet as well as such for the new merchant marine. Three naval docks which will be capable of handling the largest ships in the world are approaching completion while private companies are building similar docks under encouragement of the government in the shape of annual guarantees of dockage.

An idea of what has been accomplished with respect to ship-building is gained through the statement of Secretary Daniels, June 2, that his department had established a new world's record for rapid ship construction by the launching of the torpedo-boat destroyer *Ward*, at the Mare Island Navy Yard, California, seventeen and a half days after the keel was laid. The previous record was established shortly before that date at Camden, New Jersey, where the freighter *Tuckahoe* was launched twenty-seven days and three hours after the laying of the keel.

In 1898, twenty years ago, the first sixteen destroyers were authorized for the United States Navy. These were less than half the size of our present destroyers, and yet their average time from the laying of the keels to launching was almost exactly two years. During the ten years prior to our entrance into the present war Congress authorized an average of five or six destroyers a year. The records show that in the construction of these the average time on the ways was almost exactly eleven months, the total time of construction being about two years.

The average time on the ways of the numerous destroyers launched in 1917–18, is but little

over five months, this being somewhat less than half the average time under peace conditions. As many as 400 men were employed in work on the *Ward*, and in preparing to establish the record as much structural work as possible was prepared in advance, ready for erection and assembling before the keel was laid. While this achievement will no doubt remain unmatched for some time, it will none the less stand significant as marking a condition that is general in naval construction throughout the country, this applying to battleships and other craft as well as to destroyers.

In short, under the constructive leadership of Josephus Daniels, the navy is doing its enormous bit in a convincing manner. It took the personnel of the navy—that is, the commissioned personnel—a long time to discover the real character and personality of Mr. Daniels. It is not too much to say that many of them were hostile to his administration. But the war proved him for what he was. With administrative capacity of his own, sound judgment, and a clear brain, he was big enough to know that there were many things that had better be left to the highly trained technicians under his command.

And so in large measure he delegated many actual tasks of administration to the most competent officers in the navy, officers selected for special tasks without fear or favor. Mr. Daniels will receive, as he is now receiving, credit for their work; but he in turn is earnest in his desire so to speak and act, that this credit will be duly and properly shared by those entitled thereto. He has disregarded seniority and other departmental, not to say political factors, in choosing the right men to head the various bureaus of the Navy Department and the various units of the fleet.

He has favored the young officer, and to-day it is not too much to say that youth holds the power in the navy; but, on the other hand, he has been quick to recognize and to employ in high places the qualities that reside in officers who with years of experience, combine enduring zest and broad points of view.

In all, Secretary Daniels exemplifies the spirit of the American Navy—and the spirit of our navy is altogether consonant with our national tradition—to get into the fight and keep fighting. He has been the sponsor for a naval increase which sees our active roster increased from 56,000 men in April, 1917, to more than 400,000 at the present time, and our fighting ships increased, as already pointed out, fourfold.

And while our vessels and our fighting men are playing their part on the high seas the counsel of our trained technical experts is eagerly sought and constantly employed by the admiralties of the Allied nations. When the naval history of this war is given to the world in freest detail we shall know just how much our officers have had to do with the strategy of operations adopted by all the Entente navies. It is not violating either ethics or confidence, however, to say that our influence in this respect has been very potent and that the names of Admiral William S. Benson, chief of operations; Vice-Admiral William S. Sims, Admiral Henry T. Mayo, and Rear-Admiral Albert Gleaves are already names that are to be reckoned with abroad as at home.

As for incidents reflecting gloriously upon

the morale of our officers and men, the navy has already its growing share. There is the destroyer *Cassin* struck by a torpedo and seriously crippled, but refusing to return to port as long as there appeared to be a chance of engaging the submarine that had attacked her. There is Lieutenant Clarence C. Thomas, commander of the gun crew on the oil-ship *Vacuum*. When the ship was sunk he cheered his freezing men tossing on an icy sea in an open boat far from land, until he at length perished, his last words those of encouragement. There is Lieutenant S. F. Kalk, who swam from raft to raft encouraging and directing the survivors of the destroyer *Jacob Jones* after a torpedo had sent that vessel to the bottom. There are those two gunners on the transport *Antilles* who stood serving their gun until the ship sank and carried them down. There is the freighter *Silver-Shell* whose gun crew fought and sank the submarine that attacked the ship, and the gun crews of the *Moreni*, the *Campana*, and the *J. L. Luckenback*—indomitable heroes all. There is Osmond Kelly Ingram, who saved the *Cassin* and lost his life. There is the glorious page contributed to our naval annals, by the officers and crew of the *San Diego*. History indeed is in the making—history that Americans are proud to read.

In all that has been written in this foreword the design has been merely to sketch, to outline some of the larger achievements of the United States Navy in this war. In chapters to come our navy's course from peace into war will be followed as closely as the restrictions of a wise censorship will permit.

CHAPTER I

FIRST EXPERIENCE OF OUR NAVY WITH THE GERMAN U-BOAT—ARRIVAL OF CAPTAIN HANS ROSE AND THE U-53 AT NEWPORT—EXPERIENCES OF THE GERMAN SAILORS IN AN AMERICAN PORT—DESTRUCTION OF MERCHANTMEN BY U-53 OFF NANTUCKET—OUR DESTROYERS TO THE RESCUE—SCENES IN NEWPORT—GERMAN REJOICING—THE NAVY PREPARES FOR WAR

HOW many of us who love the sea and have followed it to greater or less extent in the way of business or pleasure have in the past echoed those famous lines of Rudyard Kipling:

> "'Good-bye Romance!' the skipper said.
> He vanished with the coal we burn."

And how often since the setting in of the grim years beginning with August of 1914 have we had occasion to appreciate the fact that of all the romance of the past ages the like to that which has been spread upon the pages of history in the past four years was never written nor imagined. Week after week there has come to us from out the veil of the maritime spaces incidents dramatic, mysterious, romantic, tragic, hideous.

Great transatlantic greyhounds whose names evoke so many memories of holiday jaunts across the great ocean slip out of port and are seen no more of men. Vessels arrive at the ports of the seven seas with tales of wanton murder, of hairbreadth escapes. Boat crews drift for days at the mercy of the seas and are finally rescued or perish man by man. The square-rigged ship once more rears its towering masts and yards above the funnels of merchant shipping; schooners brave the deep seas which never before dared leave the coastwise zones; and the sands of the West Indies have been robbed of abandoned hulks to the end that the diminishing craft of the seas be replaced. And with all there are stories of gallantry, of sea rescues, of moving incidents wherein there is nothing but good to tell of the human animal. Would that it were all so. But it is not. The ruthlessness of the German rears itself like a sordid shadow against the background of Anglo-Saxon and Latin gallantry and heroism—a diminishing shadow, thank God, and thank, also, the navy of Great Britain and of the United States.

For more than two years and a half of sea tragedy the men of our navy played the part of lookers-on. Closely following the sequence of events with the interest of men of science, there was a variety of opinion as to the desirability of our playing a part in the epic struggle on the salt water. There were officers who considered that we were well out of it; there were more who felt that our part in the struggle which the Allied nations were waging should be borne without delay. But whatever existed in the way of opinion there was no lack of unanimity in the minute study which our commissioned officers gave to the problems in naval warfare and related interests which were constantly arising in European waters.

It was not, however, until October of 1916 that the American Navy came into very close relationship with the submarine activities of the German Admiralty. The morning of October 7 of that year was one of those days for which Newport is famous—a tangy breeze sweeping over the gorse-clad cliffs and dunes that mark the environment of Bateman's Point the old yellow light-ship which keeps watch and ward over the Brenton reefs rising and falling on a cobalt sea. From out of the seaward mists there came shortly before ten o'clock a low-lying craft which was instantly picked out by the men of the light-ship as a submarine, an American submarine. There is a station for them in Newport Harbor, and submersible boats of our navy are to be found there at all times.

But as the men watched they picked up on the staff at the stern of the incoming craft the Royal German ensign. A German submarine! Be assured that enough interest in German craft of the sort had been aroused in the two years and eight months of war to insure the visitor that welcome which is born of intense interest. The submarine, the U-53, held over toward Beaver Tail and then swung into the narrow harbor entrance, finally coming to anchor off Goat Island. The commander, Captain Hans Rose, went ashore in a skiff and paid an official visit first to Rear-Admiral Austin M. Knight, commander of the Newport Naval District, and then to Rear-Admiral Albert Gleaves, chief of our destroyer flotilla.

Subsequent testimony of that German commander was that the American naval officers appeared somewhat embarrassed at the visit, suggesting men who were confronted by a situation which they were not certain how to handle. The statement of the German officer had a humorous sound and may have been humorously intended. In any event, Admiral Knight and Admiral Gleaves were very polite, and in due course paid the Germans the courtesy of a return visit. And while the submarine lay in the harbor the crew came ashore and were treated to beer by the American sailors, while crowds of curious were admitted aboard the submersible and shown about with the most open courtesy.

Captain Rose said he had come to deliver a letter to Count von Bernstorff, the German Ambassador, but such a mission seemed so trivial that rumor as to the real intentions of the craft was rife throughout the entire country. There were suspicions that she had put in for fuel, or ammunition, or supplies. But nothing to justify these thoughts occurred. The U-53 hung around through the daylight hours,

KANSAN COMPLAINS

and at sunset, with a farewell salute, put to sea.

Did our naval officers think this was the last of her? Possibly, but probably not. They knew enough of the Germans to realize, or to suspect, that their minds held little thought those days of social amenities and that such calls as were made upon neutrals contained motives which, while hidden, were none the less definite.

The night brought forth nothing, however, and the Navy Department was beginning to feel that perhaps after all the U-53 was well on her way to Germany, when early the following morning there came to the radio-station at Newport an indignant message from Captain Smith of the Hawaiian-American liner *Kansan*. He asked to know why he had been stopped and questioned by a German submarine which had halted him in the vicinity of the Nantucket light-ship at 5.30 o'clock that morning. He added that after he had convinced the submarine commander as to the nationality of his ship, he was permitted to proceed.

This looked like business, and Newport became certain of this when shortly after noon came a radio containing advices as to the sinking of the steamship *West Point* off Nantucket. Then at intervals up to midnight came other messages telling of the sinking of other vessels until the victims of the undersea craft numbered four British, a Dutch, and a Scandinavian vessel, one of them, the Halifax liner *Stephano*, a passenger-vessel, with Americans on board. Reports of vessels torpedoed, of open boats containing survivors afloat on the sea followed one another swiftly until not only Newport but the entire country was aroused.

Admiral Knight and Admiral Gleaves, who had been keeping the Navy Department at Washington in touch with every phase of the situation, beginning with the arrival of the U-53 the preceding day, lost no time in sending destroyers forth to the rescue, while already there was the cheering word that the destroyer *Balch* was on the scene and engaged in rescue work.

The departure of the destroyers was a spectacle that brought thousands of men, women, and children of Newport to the points of vantage along the shore or to small craft of all sorts

DESTROYERS TO RESCUE 33

in which they kept as close to the destroyers, preparing for their seaward flight, as they could. It was Sunday, a day when crowds were at leisure, but it was also a day when many of the officers and crew of the flotilla were on shore-leave. They were summoned from all points, however, and within a short time after the first call for help had been received the *Jarvis*, with Lieutenant L. P. Davis in command, was speeding to sea at the rate ordered by Admiral Gleaves, thirty-one knots an hour.

Inside half an hour the other destroyers shot out to sea at the same speed as the *Jarvis* while the spectators cheered them, and such as were in small boats followed until the speeding craft had disappeared. There was the *Drayton*—Lieutenant Bagley, who later was to know the venom of the German submarine—the *Ericsson*, Lieutenant-Commander W. S. Miller; the *O'Brien*, Lieutenant-Commander C. E. Courtney; the *Benham*, Lieutenant-Commander J. B. Gay; the *Cassin*, Lieutenant-Commander Vernou; the *McCall*, Lieutenant Stewart; the *Porter*, Lieutenant-Commander W. K. Wortman; the *Fanning*, Lieutenant Austin; the

Paulding, Lieutenant Douglas Howard; the *Winslow*, Lieutenant-Commander Nichols; the *Alwyn*, Lieutenant-Commander John C. Fremont; the *Cushing*, Lieutenant Kettinger; the *Cummings*, Lieutenant-Commander G. F. Neal; the *Conyngham*, Lieutenant-Commander A. W. Johnson, and the mother ship, *Melville*, Commander H. B. Price.

Soon after the destroyers had passed into the Atlantic there came a wireless message saying that twenty of the crew of the British steamship *Strathdean* had been taken on board the Nantucket light-ship. Admiral Gleaves directed the movement of his destroyers from the radio-room on the flag-ship. He figured that the run was about a hundred miles. There was a heavy sea running and a strong southwest wind. There was a mist on the ocean. It was explained by the naval authorities that the destroyers were sent out purely on a mission of rescue, and nothing was said as to any instructions regarding the enforcement of international law. None the less it was assumed, and may now be assumed, that something was said to the destroyer commanders with regard to the three-mile limit. But as to that we know no more to-day than at the time.

Suffice to say that the destroyers arrived in time not only to wander about the ocean seeking survivors in the light of a beautiful hunter's moon, but in time to witness the torpedoing of at least two merchantmen; the submarine commander, it is said, advising our war-ship commanders to move to certain locations so as not to be hit by his shells and torpedoes.

Eventually the destroyer flotilla returned with their loads of survivors and with complete details of the operations of the U-53 and, according to belief, of another submarine not designated. It appeared that the Germans were scrupulous in observing our neutrality, that their operations were conducted without the three-mile limit, and that opportunities were given crews and passengers to leave the doomed ships. There was nothing our destroyer commanders could do. Even the most hot-headed commander must have felt the steel withes of neutral obligation which held him inactive while the submarine plied its deadly work. There was, of course, nothing else to do—except to carry on the humanitarian work of rescuing victims of the U boat or boats, as the case might have been.

Later, it was given to many of the craft which set forth that October afternoon to engage in their service to humanity, to cross the seas and to meet the submarine where it lurked in the Irish Sea, the North Sea, the English Channel, and the Mediterranean. One of them, the *Cassin* was later to be struck—but not sunk—by a torpedo off the coast of England, while the *Fanning*, in company with the *Nicholson*, had full opportunity of paying off the score which most naval officers felt had been incurred when the U-53 and her alleged companion invaded American waters and sullied them with the foul deeds that had so long stained the clean seas of Europe.

German diplomats were enthusiastic over the exploits of their craft. "The U-53 and other German submarines, if there are others," said a member of the German Embassy at Washington, "is engaged in doing to the commerce of the Allies just what the British tried to do to the *Deutschland* when she left America. [The submarine *Deutschland*, engaged in commercial enterprise, had visited the United States some time previously.] It is a plain case of what is sometimes known as commerce-raiding. It is being done by submarines, that is all. Warfare, such as that which has been conducted in the Mediterranean, has been brought across the Atlantic. It should be easy to destroy more of the overseas commerce of the Allies, which is principally with America, near where it originates."

Here was a veiled threat—not so veiled either—which was no doubt marked in Washington. President Wilson received the news of the sinkings in silence, but plainly government authorities were worried over the situation. New problems were erected and the future was filled with possibilities of a multifarious nature.

Thus, within twenty-four hours it was demonstrated that the war was not 3,000 miles away from us, but close to our shores. The implied threat that it would be a simple matter for submarines to cross the Atlantic and deal with us as they were dealing with France and England and other Entente nations—not to say harmless neutrals such as Holland and Scandinavia—was not lost upon the citizens of this country. But, as usual, German judgment in the matter of psychology was astray. The threat had no effect in the way of *Schrecklichkeit*, but rather it steeled us to a future which began to appear inevitable. And deep under the surface affairs began to move in the Navy Department.

No doubt, too, the conviction began to grow upon the government that the policy of dealing fairly by Germany was not appreciated, and that when the exigencies of the war situation seemed to require it, our ships would be sent to the bottom as cheerfully as those of other neutrals such as Holland, Norway, and Sweden, as well as other countries who unfortunately were not in the positon to guard their neutrality with some show of dignity that we were in.

Subsequent events proved how true this feeling was. For not six months later the German policy of sea aggression had brought us to the point where it was not possible for us to remain out of the conflict against the pirate nation. It was in the following April that we went to war, and our first act was to send forth a destroyer flotilla to engage the U-boat in its hunting-ground. Among that flotilla, as said, were many of the craft which had rescued survivors of the Nantucket affair. They were ready and their officers were ready, nay, eager. They swept across a stormy Atlantic like unleashed hounds, and when the British commander received them at Queenstown, and asked the American commanders when they would be ready to take their places with the British destroyers, the answer came quickly:

"We are ready now."

And they were—allowing for the cleaning of a few hulls and the effecting of minor repairs to one or two of the vessels. Other destroyers remained here, of course, while a fringe of submarine-chasers and swift, armed yachts converted into government patrol-vessels were guarding our coast the day after the President signed the war resolution. But more than a year and a half was to elapse before our waters were again to know the submarine menace. Just why the Germans waited may not be known.

Probably they had all they could attend to in foreign waters. In any event it was not until June, 1918, that a coastwise schooner captain was both surprised and indignant when a shot from a craft which he took to be an American submarine went across his bows. It was not an American submarine; it was a German submersible and that schooner was sent to the bottom, followed by other wind-jammers and the Porto Rico liner *Carolina*.

Thus, what in the original instance was a test journey in the interests of German submarine activity—the visit of the U-53 in October, 1916—as well as a threat to this country bore its fruit in the development of that test trip, and in the fulfilment of that threat. At this writing the coastwise marauder, or marauders, are still off our shores, and clouds of navy craft are seeking to destroy them. We are far better equipped for such service than we were when Captain Hans Rose came here in his submarine, and it is divulging no secret information to say that this and further invasions of our home waters will be dealt with bravely and rigorously without the necessity

CONGRESS DEBATES 41

of subtracting from the number of war-vessels that are engaged with Allied fighters in maintaining commerce upon the waters of Europe.

But this is getting a bit further ahead than I intended to go at this juncture. The primary point is that with the visit of Captain Hans Rose in his undersea boat, with her depredations off our coast, the Navy Department, saying nothing to outsiders, came to accept the idea of war as something more than a possible contingency.

Debates in Congress were characterized by an increasing pointedness, and stories of sea murders increased rather than diminished. And not infrequently there were Americans on board those ships. At length came the sinking of American merchantmen and the final decision by our government to place armed guards on all merchant vessels carrying our flag. It was then that the Navy Department was called upon to take the first open steps against the German sea menace—steps rife with grim possibilities, since it operated to bring our seamen gunners into actual conflict with the German naval forces. There could be little doubt, therefore, that war would follow in inevitable course.

CHAPTER II

OUR NAVY ARMS AMERICAN MERCHANT VESSELS—DEATH OF OUR FIRST BLUEJACKET ON SERVICE IN THE WAR ZONE—VICE-ADMIRAL SIMS—WE TAKE OVER PATROL OF WATERS OF WESTERN HEMISPHERE—THE NAVAL ADVISORY BOARD OF INVENTIONS—WORK OF THIS BODY—OUR BATTLESHIPS THE LARGEST IN THE WORLD—WIDE-SPREAD OPERATIONS

ANNOUNCEMENT was made on March 12, 1917, that American merchantmen would be armed for protection against submarine attacks, and hundreds of guns of proper calibers were required for the purpose. These were taken from the vessels of the fleet and, of course, had to be replaced as soon as possible. Work was expeditiously carried forward, and hardly had the order for armed guards been issued than the American freighter *Campana* was sent to Europe well-laden with cargo and prepared to make matters interesting for any submarine that saw fit to attack by the then prevailing method of shell-fire. Other vessels soon followed, and the country witnessed the anomalous condition of the navy in war service

FIRST FATALITY

in the European war zone before war was declared.

The navy, in fact, had its first death in service before we went to war, when on April 1, John Espolucci, of Washington, D. C., one of the armed guard of the steamship *Aztec*, was killed in the course of events attending the destruction of that vessel by a submarine. By this time active hostilities had seemed inevitable and before the sinking of the *Aztec* the Navy Department had sent Admiral William S. Sims abroad to get in touch with the British and French Admiralties for the purpose of discussing the most effective participation of our war-ships in the conflict. Later, when war was actually declared, Sims was promoted to vice-admiral, and made commander of the United States naval forces operating in European waters.

No better man for this post could have been selected. A graduate of the Naval Academy in the class of 1880, his career in the navy had been one sequence of brilliant achievement. As naval attaché at Paris and Petrograd, in the course of his distinguished service he had ample opportunities for the study of European naval conditions, and later he was intrusted with the important duty of developing gunnery practice and marksmanship in our battle-fleet. The immense value of his work in this respect is an open book. His instincts were wholly scientific, and with neither fear nor favor he carried forward our record for marksmanship until it was second to that of no navy in the world. The one mark upon his record is an indiscreet speech made in London, before the European War occurred, in which he stated that blood was thicker than water, and that at the necessary moment the navies of the United States and of Great Britain would be found joined in brotherly co-operation. England liked that speech a lot, but Germany did not, and Washington was rather embarrassed. Beginning, however, with April of 1917, that speech delivered several years previously was recalled as perfectly proper, pat, and apropos.

There can be no doubt that his constructive advice, suggestion, and criticism were of enormous benefit to the British and the French, and by the same token exceedingly harmful

SIMS IN COMMAND 45

to the murderous submarine campaign of Germany. As evidence of the regard in which the admiralty of Great Britain held this American officer, witness the fact that upon one occasion when the British commander-in-chief of naval operations on the Irish coast was compelled to leave his command for a period, Admiral Sims was nominated by the admiralty to serve as chief of the combined forces until the British commander returned.

But this mission of Admiral Sims, and the eventual despatch of submarine flotillas to the war zone, were but two phases of the enormous problem which confronted the Navy Department upon the outbreak of hostilities. There was first of all the task of organizing and operating the large transport system required to carry our share of troops overseas for foreign service. Within a month after the President had announced that troops would be sent to Europe the first contingent had been organized, and all its units were safely landed in France before the 4th of July. These included a force of marines under Colonel (now Brigadier-General) Charles A. Doyen, which is serving in the army under

Major-General Pershing. Since that time a constant stream of troops and supplies has poured across the Atlantic under naval control and supervision, the presiding officer in charge of transport being Rear-Admiral Albert Gleaves.

Then, again, the United States took over control of most of the patrol of the western Atlantic. Our thousands of miles of coast had to be guarded against enemy attack and protected against German raiders. A squadron under command of Admiral William B. Caperton was sent to South America and received with the utmost enthusiasm at Rio de Janeiro, at Montevideo and Buenos Aires, which cities were visited on invitation from the governments of Brazil, Uruguay, and Argentina. After Brazil's entrance into the war the Brazilian Navy co-operated with our vessels in the patrol of South American waters.

The taking over of some 800 craft of various kinds, and their conversion into types needed, provided the navy with the large number of vessels required for transports, patrol service, submarine-chasers, mine-sweepers, mine-layers, tugs, and other auxiliaries. The repair of the 109 German ships whose machinery had been damaged by their crews—details of which will be treated in a subsequent chapter—added more than 700,000 tons to our available naval and merchant tonnage, and provided for the navy a number of huge transports which have been in service for nearly a year. Hundreds of submarine-chasers have now been built, and a number of destroyers and other craft completed and placed in service. The first merchant ship to be armed was the oil-tanker *Campana;* guns manned by navy men were on board when she sailed for Europe, March 12, 1917. The big American passenger-liners *St. Paul* and *New York* were armed on March 16 of that year, and the Red Star liner *Kroonland* and the *Mongolia* on March 19. And continuously up to the present writing merchant ships as they have become available have been armed and provided with navy gun crews. Since the arming of the *Campana* more than 1,300 vessels have been furnished with batteries, ammunition, spare parts, and auxiliaries.

But of equal importance, greater importance

history may decree it, was Secretary Daniels's action in 1915 of appointing the Naval Advisory Board of Inventions. That was looking ahead with a vengeance. The idea was to make available the latent inventive genius of the country to improve the navy. The plan adopted by Secretary Daniels for selecting this extraordinary board included a request to the eleven great engineering and scientific societies of the country to select by popular election two members to represent their society on the board. Results were immediately gratifying. Nominations were forthcoming at once, and in September of 1915 the board, which came popularly to be known as the Inventions Board, met in Washington for organization. Thomas A. Edison was selected by the Secretary of the Navy as chairman of the board, and the other members were elected as follows:

From the American Chemical Society: W. R. Whitney, director of Research Laboratory, General Electric Company, where he has been the moving spirit in the perfection of metallic electric-lamp filaments and the development of wrought tungsten. L. H. Baekeland, founder of the Nepera Chemical Company and inventor of photographic paper.

From the American Institute of Electrical Engineers: Frank Julian Sprague, consulting engineer for Sprague, Otis, and General Electric Companies and concerned in the establishment of the first electrical trolley systems in this country. B. G. Lamme, chief engineer of the Westinghouse Electric and Manufacturing Company and a prolific inventor.

From the American Mathematical Society: Robert Simpson Woodward, president of the Carnegie Institution and an authority on astronomy, geography, and mathematical physics. Arthur Gordon Webster, professor of physics at Clark University and an authority on sound, its production and measurement.

From the American Society of Civil Engineers: Andrew Murray Hunt, consulting engineer, experienced in the development of hydroelectric, steam, and gas plants. Alfred Craven, chief engineer of Public Service Commission, New York, and formerly division engineer in charge of construction work on Croton aqueduct and reservoirs.

From the American Aeronautical Society: Mathew Bacon Sellers, director of Technical Board of the American Aeronautical Society and the first to determine dynamic wind-pressure on arched surfaces by means of "wind funnel." Hudson Maxim, ordnance and explosive expert, maker of the first smokeless powder adopted by the United States Government.

The Inventors' Guild: Peter Cooper Hewitt, inventor of electric lamp, appliances to enable direct-current apparatus to be used with alternating-current circuits, and devices for telephones and aircraft. Thomas Robbins, president of Robbins Conveying Belt Company and inventor of many devices for conveying coal and ore.

From American Society of Automobile Engineers: Andrew L. Riker, vice-president of Locomobile Company, electrical and mechanical engineer and inventor of many automobile devices. Howard E. Coffin, vice-president of Hudson Motor Car Company and active in the development of internal-combustion engines.

MANY BODIES INVOLVED

From the American Institute of Mining Engineers: William Laurence Saunders, chairman of the Board of Directors of the Ingersoll-Rand Company and inventor of many devices for subaqueous and rock drilling. Benjamin Bowditch Thayer, president of the Anaconda Copper Mining Company and an authority on explosives.

From the American Electro Chemical Society: Joseph William Richards, professor of Electro-Chemistry at Lehigh and author of numerous works on electrometallurgy. Lawrence Addicks, consulting engineer for Phelps, Dodge and Company and authority on the metallurgy of copper.

American Society of Mechanical Engineers: William Leroy Emmet, engineer with the General Electric Company. He designed and perfected the development of the Curtis Turbine and was the first serious promotor of electric propulsion for ships. Spencer Miller, inventor of ship-coaling apparatus and the breeches-buoy device used in rescues from shipwrecks.

From the American Society of Aeronautic Engineers: Henry Alexander Wise Wood, engineer and manufacturer of printing-machinery and student of naval aeronautics. Elmer Ambrose Sperry, founder of Sperry Electric Company, designer of electric appliances and gyroscope stabilizer for ships and airplanes.

Just what service this board has performed is in the keeping of the government. But that it has been a distinguished service we may not doubt. Seated in their headquarters at Washington, their minds centred upon the various problems of the sea which the war brought forth, they have unquestionably exerted a constructive influence no less vital than that played by the officers and men of the navy on the fighting front. Only one announcement ever came from this board, and that was when William L. Saunders gave forth the statement that a means of combating the submarine had been devised. This early in the war. Doubt as to the strict accuracy of the statement came from other members of the Inventions Board, and then the whole matter was hushed. Mr. Saunders said nothing more and neither did his colleagues.

But whether emanating from the lucubrations of Mr. Edison's board, or wherever devised, we know that the American Navy has applied many inventions to the work of combating the under-sea pirate. A type of depth-bomb was developed and applied. This is one of the most efficient methods of beating the submarine that has yet been found. Explosive charges are fitted with a mechanism designed to explode the charge at a predetermined depth below the surface of the sea. The force of the explosion of a depth charge dropped close to a submarine is sufficient to disable if not sink it, and American boats have been fitted with various interesting means of getting these bombs into the water.

Smoke-producing apparatus was developed to enable a vessel to conceal herself behind a smoke-screen when attacked by submarines and thus escape. Several types of screen have been invented and applied in accordance with the character of the vessel. After a study of the various types of mines in existence, there was produced an American mine believed to involve all the excellent points of mines of whatever nationality, while another extraordinary invention was the non-ricochet projectile. The ordinary pointed projectile striking the water almost horizontally is deflected and ricochets. A special type of shell which did not glance off the surface of the ocean was developed early in 1917 and supplied to all vessels sailing in the war zone.

The first year of the war saw also the development of the seaplane, with the adaption to this vehicle of the air a nonrecoil gun, which permits the use of comparatively large calibers, and of the Lewis gun. This year saw also the completion of the latest type of naval 16-inch gun, throwing a projectile weighing 2,100 pounds. Our newest battleships will mount them. In this connection it is interesting to note that broadside weights have tripled in the short space of twenty years; that the total weight of steel thrown by a single broadside of the *Pennsylvania* to-day is 17,508 pounds, while the total weight thrown from the broadside of the *Oregon* of Spanish-American War fame was 5,600 pounds.

The navy also went in vigorously for aviation and has done exceedingly well. After the ex-

SPECIALIZED ACTIVITIES 55

pansion of private plants had been provided for, the navy decided to operate a factory of its own, and a great building 400 by 400 feet was erected in Philadelphia in 110 days at a cost of $700,000. Contracts involving approximately $1,600,000 have been made which will more than treble the capacity of this plant.

In addition to work of this sort and services including scores of specialized activities, such as medical development, ordnance and munitions manufacture, building of yards, docks, and all sorts of accessory facilities, the navy before the war had been a month under way had given contracts for the construction of several hundred submarine-chasers, having a length of 110 feet and driven by three 220-horse-power gasolene-engines, to thirty-one private firms and six navy-yards. All of these craft are now in service, and have done splendidly both in meeting stormy seas and in running down the submarines. While the British prefer a smaller type of submarine-chaser, they have no criticism of ours. Many of these 110-footers, built of wood, crossed the ocean in weather which did considerable damage to larger craft, and yet were practically unscathed. The French are using many of them.

Another larger type of chaser, corresponding to the destroyer, is the patrol-boat of the *Eagle* class built at the plant of Henry Ford in Detroit.

The most recent battleships laid down by the navy are the largest ever attempted. The biggest British battleship of which we have knowledge displaces 27,500 tons; the largest German, 28,448 metric tons (28,000 American tons), while the largest Japanese battleship displaces 30,600 tons. These may be compared with our *Arizona* and *Pennsylvania*, 31,400 tons; *Idaho*, *Mississippi*, and *New Mexico*, 32,000 tons; *California* and *Tennessee* 32,300 tons, *Colorado*, *Washington*, *Maryland*, and *West Virginia*, 32,600 tons, while six new battleships authorized early in the present year are designed to be 41,500 tons. Our new battle-cruisers of 35,000 tons and 35 knots speed will be the swiftest in the world, having a speed equal to the latest and fastest destroyers. They will also be the largest in the world with the exception of the

CIVILIAN EMPLOYES

four British battle-cruisers of the *Hood* class, which are 41,200 tons.

On April 1, 1917, the total number of civilian employees in the nine principal navy-yards was 29,708. On March 1, 1918, the total number of employees in the same yards was 58,026. The total number of mechanics now employed at all navy yards and stations throughout the country is more than 66,000.

The Navy Powder Factory at Indianapolis, Ind., manufactures powder of the highest grade for use in the big guns; it employs 1,000 men and covers a square mile. Additional buildings and machinery, together with a new generating-plant, are now being installed. The torpedo-station at Newport, a large plant where torpedoes are manufactured, has been greatly enlarged and its facilities in the way of production radically increased. Numerous ammunition-plants throughout the country prepare the powder charge, load and fuse the shell, handle high explosives, and ship the ammunition to vessels in the naval service. Among recent additions to facilities is an automatic mine-loading plant of great capacity and new design.

Schools of various sorts, ranging from those devoted to the teaching of wireless telegraphy to cooking, were established in various parts of the country, and from them a constant grist of highly specialized men are being sent to the ships and to stations.

In these, and in numerous ways not here mentioned, the Navy Department signalized its entrance into the war. While many new fields had to be entered—with sequential results in way of mistakes and delays—there were more fields, all important, wherein constructive preparation before we entered the war were revealed when the time came to look for practical results.

CHAPTER III

FIRST HOSTILE CONTACT BETWEEN THE NAVY AND THE GERMANS—ARMED GUARDS ON MERCHANT VESSELS—"CAMPANA" FIRST TO SAIL—DANIELS REFUSES OFFER OF MONEY AWARDS TO MEN WHO SINK SUBMARINES—"MONGOLIA" SHOWS GERMANY HOW THE YANKEE SAILORMAN BITES—FIGHT OF THE "SILVERSHELL"—HEROISM OF GUNNERS ON MERCHANT SHIPS—SINKING OF THE "ANTILLES"—EXPERIENCES OF VOYAGERS

IN the way of direct hostile contact between the Navy Department and Germany we find the first steps taken in the placing of armed naval-guards on American merchantmen. While this was authorized by the government before war was declared, it was recognized as a step that would almost inevitably lead to our taking our part in the European conflict and the nation, as a consequence, prepared its mind for such an outcome of our new sea policy. Germany had announced her policy of unrestricted submarine warfare in February, 1917, and on Feburary 10 of that month two American steamships, the *Orleans* and the *Rochester*, left port for France in defiance of the German warning. Both vessels were unarmed and both arrived safely on the other side—the *Rochester* was subsequently sunk—but their sailing without any means of defense against attack aroused the nation and spurred Congress to action.

On March 12 the first armed American merchantman, the *Campana*, left port with a gun mounted astern, and a crew of qualified naval marksmen to man it. In the following October Secretary Daniels announced that his department had found guns and crews for every one of our merchant vessels designated for armament and that the guards consisted of from sixteen to thirty-two men under command of commissioned or chief petty officers of the navy. When the work of finding guns for vessels was begun the navy had few pieces that were available. While there were many fine gunners in the naval force, there were not a sufficient number of them to enable the quick arming of merchantmen without handicapping the war-ships.

So every battleship in the navy was converted into a school of fire to train men for the duty, and the naval ordnance plants entered

REWARDS OFFERED 61

upon the work of turning out guns qualified for service on merchant craft. There were guns in stock, as a matter of fact, but the number was insufficient for the purpose in hand because, before the submarine developed a new sort of sea warfare, it was not the policy of the nations to arm merchant vessels other than those used as naval auxiliaries. But, as already said, so expeditiously were affairs carried on that some six months after the decision to equip our freighters and passenger-liners with means of protection we had the sailors and the guns necessary to meet all demands.

The following telegraphic correspondence, between two St. Louis business men and the Secretary of the Navy, gives a very fair idea of the spirit in which the citizens of this country accepted the decision of the government to arm our merchant marine:

"ST. LOUIS, MO., April 11, 1917.
"*Hon. Josephus Daniels, Secretary of the Navy, Washington, D. C.*
"We will pay $500 to the captain and crew of the first American merchant ship to destroy

a hostile submarine after this date. Money will be paid on award by your office."

"BENJAMIN GRATZ.
"ANDERSON GRATZ."

To which Mr. Daniels replied as follows:

"I thank you for the spirit which prompted your offer. It is my distinct feeling that money rewards for such bravery is not in keeping with the spirit of our day."

And neither it was. The American naval men were intent upon duty and their duty was merely to protect the dignity as well as the safety of our sea-borne commerce. The mercenary element was absent and that Mr. Daniels did well to emphasize this fact was the conviction of the navy as well as of the entire country; while, at the same time, as the secretary said, the spirit underlying the offer was appreciated.

In the meantime the German Government—which no doubt had not expected such drastic action on the part of the United States—was profoundly disturbed, and it was stated that crews of American merchantmen who ventured to fire upon German submarines before a state of war existed between the two countries must expect to meet the fate of the British merchant captain, Charles Fryatt, who, as will be recalled, was tried and executed in Germany for attempting to ram the German submarine 7-33 with his vessel, the Great Eastern Railway steamship, *Brussels*, in July of 1916. This warning set forth in the *Neueste Nachrichten*, of Munich, is so ingenious that the reader interested in Teutonic pyschology will no doubt be interested in the perusal thereof.

"We assume," the newspaper said, "that President Wilson realizes the fate to which he is subjecting his artillerymen. According to the German prize laws it is unneutral support of the enemy if a neutral ship takes part in hostilities. If such a ship opposes the prize-court then it must be treated as an enemy ship. The prize rules specify as to the crews of such ships. If, without being attached to the forces of the enemy, they take part in hostilities or make forcible resistance, they may be treated according to the usages of war. If President

Wilson, knowing these provisions of international law, proceeds to arm American merchantmen he must assume responsibility for the eventuality that American seamen will meet the fate of Captain Fryatt."

All of which did not appear to frighten our government one bit. We set ourselves to the task of equipping our merchant craft with seamen-gunners and guns, and it was not long—April 25, in fact—before an incident occurred that brought forth a chuckle from Colonel Roosevelt, a chuckle accompanied by the historic remark: "Thank heaven! Americans have at last begun to hit. We have been altogether too long at the receiving end of this war that Germany has been waging upon us."

This ebullition was occasioned by the report of the first real American blow of the war when, late in April, 1917, the crack American freighter *Mongolia* showed the German Navy that the time had arrived when the long, strong arm of Uncle Sam was reaching out a brawny fist over the troubled waters of the Atlantic.

The *Mongolia* had left an American port after war had been declared, and she was guarded by a 6-inch gun, with a crew of seamen-gunners under command of Lieutenant Bruce Ware. Captain Emery Rice commanded the freighter, and the voyage across the Atlantic had proceeded without incident until the port of destination, an English port, lay just twenty-four hours away. In other words, the *Mongolia* was in the war zone. The sea was untroubled, and the gun crew gathered at their stations and the lookouts on mast and deck were beginning to believe that the trip would end as uneventfully as it had begun. No doubt there was some disappointment in this thought; for, strange as it may seem, our armed freighters were rather inclined to hunt out the submarines than to dodge them. It has been the frequent testimony that our armed guards are always spoiling for fight, not seeking to avoid it.

At all events, the freighter steamed through the light mists of the April afternoon—it was the anniversary of the battle of Lexington—and Captain Rice, who had been five days in his clothes, and Lieutenant Ware of the navy and his nineteen men, serving the two 4-inch forward guns and the 6-inch stern piece, casting their eyes over the vast stretch of water when at 5.30 o'clock the gruff voice of the first mate, who had been peering over the dodger rail of the bridge rumbled over the vessel.

"Submarine. Two points off the port bow."

There it was, sure enough, a periscope at least, practically dead ahead, her position with relation to the *Mongolia* being such that the vessel offered a narrow target, a target hardly worth the wasting of a valuable torpedo. No, the submarine was either waiting for a broadside expanse or else was intent upon a gunfight.

Lieutenant Ware and his seamen were ready. In compliance to a sharply spoken order the three guns were turned upon the periscope. But quick as the gunners were, the submarine was quicker, and as the guns were brought to bear the periscope sank gently out of sight. Captain Rice almost pulled the engine-room signal telegraph-lever out by its roots in bringing the ship to full speed toward the spot where the periscope had last been seen, his idea of course, being to ram the lurking craft.

For two minutes nothing was seen and then

a shout from one of the lookouts heralded the reappearance of the submersible, this time a thousand yards to port, the *Mongolia* offering to the Germans a fair broadside expanse of hull. Lieutenant Ware's voice arose and the next instant the 6-inch piece spoke. That periscope went into splinters; a direct hit. Watchers on the freighter saw the shell strike its mark fairly. A great geyser arose from the sea, and when it died there were evidences of commotion beneath the surface. Then gradually foam and oil spread upon the gentle waves.

There was no doubt about the hit. Lieutenant Ware knew before the shell struck that the aim had been accurate. There was no guesswork about it. It was a case of pure mathematics. The whole affair was over in two minutes. The vessel did not stop to reconnoitre, but steamed away at full speed, sending ahead wireless reports of the fight against the undersea craft. The British naval officers who came bounding across the waters on their destroyers were extremely complimentary in their praise, and when the *Mongolia* returned to New York there was a dinner in honor of Lieutenant Ware, an expression of the lingering emotions which had fired the nation when word of the incident was cabled to this country. Since that fight the Germans, enraged, seem to have marked the *Mongolia;* for in succeeding months she was set upon repeatedly by the submarine flotilla, seeking revenge for her temerity in sending one of their number to the bottom. But she is still afloat and ready for anything that comes out of the sea.

None the less, the government began to feel that it would be wiser not to mention the names of ships engaged with submarines, and thus when the next good fight occurred the name of the vessel engaged was not given. Aside from hoping thus to keep a vessel from being marked it had been the experience of the British Government that when Germans had identified captured sailors as having belonged to vessels that had sunk or damaged submarines they subjected them to unusual severity. Our navy wished to avoid this in the case of our men.

However, the name of the vessel which engaged in a fight on May 30, was given out the day after the Washington report by the French Ministry of Marine. It was the *Silvershell*, commanded by Captain Tom Charlton with a gun crew commanded by William J. Clark, a warrant-officer from the battleship *Arkansas*. The battle occurred on May 30, in the Mediterranean and in addition to strength added by an efficient gun crew, whose commander, Clark, had been a turret captain on the *Arkansas*, the *Silvershell* was an extremely fast ship. As a consequence, when the submarine poked her nose out of the Mediterranean blue, expecting easy prey, she found confronting her a man's-size battle. In all sixty shots were exchanged, and the submarine not only beaten off, but sunk with the twenty-first shot fired from the *Silvershell*. It was a great fight, and Clark was recommended for promotion.

While the government jealously guarded details of this and subsequent fights, the country had adequate food for pride in such announcements from the Navy Department as that of July 26, when certain gun-crew officers were cited for promotion and an outline of reasons therefor set forth.

There was Andrew Copassaki, chief boatswain's mate, for instance, who was transferred from the battleship *Arkansas* to take charge of the gun crew of the steamship *Moreni*. He commanded this crew when the *Moreni* was sunk by a German submarine on the morning of June 12. This gun crew put up a fight on the deck of that sinking vessel which was so gallant as to elicit words of praise from the commander of the attacking submarine. Copassaki, when the ship was in flames, from shellfire, rushed through the fire to the forward gun and continued to serve it against the submarine until the gun was put completely out of commission. This gallant hero was born in Greece, and had been in the navy twenty years.

Then there was Harry Waterhouse, a chief turret captain, transferred from the dreadnought *New York* to command the armed crew of the *Petrolite* which was sunk by a U-boat on June 10. The vessel sank so rapidly after being torpedoed that the guns could not be used. The navy men, however, under the command of Waterhouse, assisted in getting

LOSS OF *PETROLITE* 71

out the boats and lowering them and getting the crew to safety, to a man—although the *Petrolite* went over on her beam ends in less than a minute. No member of the armed guard left the sinking vessel until ordered to do so by Waterhouse. These are but a few of the instances of signal gallantry which have filled the records of our navy since we entered the war.

And while our merchant crews were thus at work the navy was busy sending soldiers to the other side. Not a mishap had occurred on the eastbound traffic—and at this writing none has yet occurred—but on October 17, the transport *Antilles*, which had made several safe journeys with soldiers destined for General Pershing's expeditionary forces, was torpedoed and sunk when homeward bound with a loss of 70 lives out of 237 men on board. The transport was sunk while under the convoy of American naval patrol-vessels, and she had on board the usual armed gun crew.

Not only was the *Antilles* the first American Army transport to be lost in the present war, but she was the first vessel under American convoy to be successfully attacked. She was well out to sea at the time and the convoy of protecting vessels was smaller for this reason, and for the fact that she was westbound, carrying no troops. The submarine was never seen and neither was the torpedo. There has been rumor that the explosion that sank her came from the inside, but so far as any one knows this is merely port gossip of such nature as arises when vessels are lost. Our second transport to be lost was the *President Lincoln*, taken over from the Germans when war was declared. She, too, was eastbound, well out to sea, and the loss of life was small. The third was the *Covington*, formerly the German liner *Cincinnati*, which was torpedoed in the early summer of this year while on her way to an American port.

Life on merchantmen, freighters, liners, and the like, crossing the Atlantic, has been fraught with peril and with excitement ever since we went into the war. Even with armed guards there are of course all sorts of chances of disaster, chances frequently realized; but, on the other hand, in a great majority of cases the vessels of the transatlantic passenger service have crossed to and fro, giving their passengers all the thrills of an exciting situation without subjecting them to anything more serious.

Let me quote in part a letter from a Princeton man, Pleasants Pennington, who was a passenger on the French transatlantic liner *Rochambeau*, on one of its trips late in 1917.

"What about the submarines? They haven't put in an appearance yet. We haven't worried about them because we only got into the war zone last night; but I may have more to write about before we get into Bordeaux on Wednesday or Thursday. There are several people on board—especially ladies of the idle rich—who have been much concerned about the safety of the ship and incidentally their own skins. . . . The Frenchmen, the officers of the ship and especially the captain (his name is Joam) take a very philosophic view of the situation, and shrug their shoulders with Gallic fatalism. If they shall be torpedoed—*tant pis!* But why worry? . . . I had a talk with our captain the second day out, and he seemed to have made a pretty thorough study of tactics for avoiding submarines. He said they did not go more than 800 miles from land, and that the best protection is to go fast and keep one's eyes open. The *Rochambeau* had two beautiful new 6-inch guns mounted on the stern and a 3-inch gun in the bow. . . . As near as I can gather, our tactics seem to be to keep a lookout ahead and trust to getting a shot at any submarine that shows its head before it can launch a torpedo. I believe torpedoes are not accurate at over a mile, and the speed of a submarine is only nine knots while ours is nineteen. . . . I think the most distinctive feature of war-time travel is the fact that the boat must be perfectly dark at night to an outside observer. This rule is observed on the entire voyage, and results in heavy iron shutters being bolted on all port-holes and windows as soon as dusk falls so that the entire atmosphere of the cabins, smoking-room, reading-rooms, etc., becomes very vile in a surprisingly short time after dark. . . . We now sleep on deck and are very comfortable. The deck is crowded at night with people of different ages, sexes, and nationalities, sleeping in the most charming confusion and proximity."

Well, the *Rochambeau* arrived without untoward incident as she had done so often before and has done since. Another letter is that of a Yale senior, enlisted in the navy and one of the crew of a transport. "We looked very formidable as we steamed out of the harbor. An armored cruiser led the way and on either side a torpedo destroyer. . . . We proceed very cautiously. After sunset all lights go out. There is no smoking anywhere on board and not a light even in the stateroom. Then if we look out we see the other ships of the convoy— we hug one another closely—just stumbling through the water like phantom shapes—and that's the weirdest sight I have ever seen. . . . To-day we are having gun practice on board the transport—trial shots for the subs and the cruiser experimenting with balloon observers. Such are our interests. . . . Last night I had a wonderful experience. It was delightful— one of those that tickle my masculine pride. I was detailed in charge of a watch in the forward crow's-nest—a basket-like affair on the very top of the foremast about 150 feet from the water. . . . From the nest you get a wonderful view—a real bird's-eye view—for the men walking on the deck appear as pigmies, and the boats following in our trail look like dories. Our duty is to watch with powerful glasses for any traces of periscopes, and we are connected up with telephones to the gunners who are always ready for the 'call' and eager for action. This is only the first of the thrilling experiences which I expect, or, rather, hope to have." But that convoy arrived safely, too.

The convoy, by the way, was largely an American idea, a departure from the policy of protecting a single vessel. A group of craft about to cross, sometimes as many as a score or more, are sent forth together under adequate protection of destroyers and cruisers. At night towing-disks are dropped astern. These are white and enable the rearward vessels to keep their distance with relation to those steaming ahead. The destroyers circle in and about the convoyed craft, which, in the meantime, are describing zigzag courses in order that submarines may not be able to calculate their gun or torpedo fire with any degree of accuracy.

The destroyers shoot in front of bows and

LOSS OF THE *TUSCANIA*

around sterns with impunity, leaving in their trail a phosphorescent wake. Sometimes in the case of a fast liner the destroyers, what with the high speed of the craft they are protecting and the uncertain course, narrowly escape disaster. As a matter of fact, one of them, the American destroyer *Chauncey*, was lost in this manner. But she is the only one.

Here is a letter from a Yale man, a sailor, which contains rather a tragic story, the loss of the transport *Tuscania* under British convoy:

"I could see a lighthouse here and there on the Irish and Scotch shores, and though I knew there were plenty of ships about not one was to be seen. (It was night, of course). All at once I saw a dull flare and a moment after a heavy boom. Then about half a mile away the *Tuscania* stood out in the glare of all the lights suddenly turned on. I could see her painted funnels and the sides clear and distinct against the dark. Another boom and the lights and the ship herself vanished. The next instant lights and rockets began to go up, red and white, and from their position I knew they must be from the *Tuscania* and that she was falling out of the convoy. Then came a crash of guns and a heavier shock that told of depth-bombs and the blaze of a destroyer's searchlights—gone again in an instant—and then absolute silence."

The sinking of the *Antilles* was followed—October 25, 1917—by an announcement that thereafter bluejackets would man and naval officers command all transports. Up to that time, while there had been naval guards on the transports, the crews and officers of ships had been civilians. It was believed that highly disciplined naval men would be more effective than the constantly shifting crews of civilians. So it has proved.

CHAPTER IV

DESTROYERS ON GUARD—PREPARATIONS OF FLOTILLA TO CROSS THE OCEAN—MEETING THE "ADRIATIC"—FLOTILLA ARRIVES IN QUEENSTOWN—RECEPTION BY BRITISH COMMANDER AND POPULACE—"WE ARE READY NOW, SIR"—ARRIVAL OF THE FAMOUS CAPTAIN EVANS ON THE AMERICAN FLAG-SHIP—OUR NAVY A WARM-WEATHER NAVY—LOSS OF THE "VACUUM"

WHEN we entered the war the Navy Department had one definite idea concerning its duty with regard to the submarine. It was felt that it was more necessary to deal drastically with this situation than to meet it merely by building a large fleet of cargo-carrying vessels in the hope that a sufficient number of them would escape the U-boats to insure the carrying of adequate food and supplies to France and the British Isles. The view was taken that, while the ship-building programme was being carried out—there was of course no idea of not furthering the policy embodied in the plea of the British statesman for ships, ships and yet more ships—means should be taken of driving the submarine from the seas.

We held the attitude that the nation which

had given to the world a weapon so formidable as the undersea fighter had within it the ability to devise a means of combating it successfully. And, as a matter of fact, long before we went into the conflict the Navy Department had not ignored consideration of ways and means in this respect. As a consequence, when the British and French War Commissions arrived in this country they found our naval officers bristling with ideas, some of them apparently so feasible that the British naval representatives were both pleased and astonished.

We do not know all that passed between the Americans and the British with regard to the submarine, but this we do know: that the British went back to England with a greater respect for our powers of constructive thought than they had when they reached this country. Among some of the early suggestions was the sowing of contact mines in waters through which the submarines would be obliged to pass in leaving and entering their bases. Then there was the scheme of protecting vessels in groups, and other excellent ideas which were soon put into effect.

Immediately after the signing of the war resolution by President Wilson the Navy Department proceeded to put various plans into execution. At 9.30 o'clock one warm April night commanders of various destroyers in service along the coast received orders to proceed at daylight to the home navy-yards and fit out with all despatch for distant service. None of the officers knew what was ahead, not definitely, that is; but all knew that the future held action of vital sort and with all steam the venomous gray destroyers were soon darting up and down the coast toward their various navy-yards, at Boston, New York, and elsewhere.

Arriving here, the vessels went at once into dry dock while a force of men who were in waiting proceeded to clean and paint the hulls, while stores and provisions to last three months were assembled. In a few days the flotilla set forth. No commander knew where he was going. Instructions were to proceed to a point fifty miles east of Cape Cod, and there to open sealed instructions. One may imagine the thoughts of the officers and crews of the sea-fighters—which above all other craft had signally demonstrated the fact that they and they alone were qualified to bring the fear of God, as the navy saying is, to the Germans—as they ploughed through the seas to the point where orders might be opened and the way ahead made clear.

"And when," said a destroyer commander, speaking of that trip, "I got to the designated point at midnight, I opened my orders and found that we were to make for Queenstown. You may be sure I breathed a fervent cheer, for I had been itching for a crack at the sub ever since certain events off Nantucket the preceding fall."

The flotilla took ten days in making the journey, the time thus consumed being due to a southeast gale which accompanied the boats for the first seven days of the journey. There were various incidents, but nothing of the dramatic save the picking up and escorting of the big British liner *Adriatic*, and later the meeting 300 miles off the Irish coast of the brave little British destroyer *Mary Rose*, which had been sent out to meet the Americans. The *Mary Rose*, by the way, was sunk three months later by a German raider. The commander of the *Mary Rose* assured the Americans that they would be welcome and that their co-operation would be highly appreciated.

One may fancy so. Things were looking exceedingly black about that time. In the previous three weeks submarines had sunk 152 British merchant vessels, and patrol-vessels each day were bringing in survivors of the various victims. It was a situation which could not go on if the British cause were not to be very seriously injured. The question of supplies, food, munitions, and the like, for which both France and England were relying upon the United States to furnish, was looming vitally. This country had the things to send, all cargoes, of all sorts. But to send them to the war zone and then have them lost was a heart-breaking situation for every one concerned.

One thus is able to imagine the emotions with which the British at Queenstown received our flotilla when it came in from the sea on the morning of May 13. Motion pictures of this eventful arrival have been shown in this country, with the result that we who were not there have an impression of a crowded waterfront, of American flags flying everywhere, of the American commander leaving his vessel and going ashore to call upon the British commander Admiral Sir Lewis Bayly and the Honorable Wesley Frost, the American Consul at Queenstown. The destroyers had steamed into the harbor in a long line and with great precision came to a stop at the designated moorings. All this, as said, we have seen on the film, as we have seen the British and American officers going through the motions of formal felicitation. What was said, however, came to us through another medium. Admiral Bayly, after the formal ceremony of greeting was ended, said with British directness:

"When will you be ready for business?"

The reply was prompt:

"We can start at once, sir."

Admiral Bayly did not attempt to conceal his surprise, but he made no comment until after he had completed a tour of the various American craft. Then he turned to the American commander:

"You were right about being prepared."

CAPTAIN EVANS

"Yes," returned the American; "we made preparations in the course of the trip over. That is why we are ready."

"Very good," smiled the British commander. "You are a fine body of men and your boats look just as fit." As a matter of fact, while all equipment was found to be in excellent condition and the men ready and eager to go out after submarines, it was deemed best to send one or two of the craft to dry dock to have their hulls inspected and, if necessary, shorn of all barnacles or other marine growth that might have become attached to the plating on the journey across.

In the meantime had occurred a very pretty incident which is now one of the stock stories in the ward-rooms of British and American sea-fighters in European waters. It seems that not long before the destroyers were due to arrive Captain Edward R. G. R. Evans, C. B., who was second in command of the Scott Antarctic Expedition, came up the Thames on board his battered destroyer, the *Broke*. Now, the *Broke* on the night of April 20, off Dover, had been engaged in an action which stands as one of the glorious achievements at arms in the annals of sea-fighting. The *Broke* that night was attacked by six German destroyers and, after a battle characterized by bulwark rasping against bulwark, by boarding-parties, hand-to-hand fighting, and all the elements that make the pages of Mayne Reid thrilling, defeated the six destroyers and proceeded to port with flags flying.

With all this in mind the admiralty decided to pay the Americans the distinguished compliment of attaching Captain Evans to the American flag-ship as a sort of liaison officer. So when the American flotilla was reported, the British hero set forth and in good time boarded the flag-ship of the flotilla. He was accompanied by a young aide, and both were received with all courtesy by the American commander. But the British aide could see that the American had not associated his visitor with the man whose laurels were still fresh not only as an explorer but as a fighter.

There was talk of quarters for Captain Evans, and the American commander seemed doubtful just where to put his guest. Finally he sent the British officer below with a lieutenant to see what could be done. When the two had disappeared Evans's aide turned to the American commander.

"I don't think," he said, flushing rather diffidently, that you quite grasped just who you have on board, and then with great distinctness he added: "He is R. G. R. Evans. He——"

There came an exclamation from the American, and stepping forward he seized the young officer by the shoulders.

"Do you mean to say that he is Evans of the *Broke?*" he cried.

As the Briton nodded and was about to speak, the American leaped from his side, made the companion-ladder, and fairly tumbled below. Approaching Captain Evans, he said:

"Captain Evans, my apologies; I didn't quite place you at first. I merely wish to tell you now not to worry about quarters. I say this because you are going to have my bunk—and I—I am going to sleep on the floor."

And here is a little incident which occurred when the destroyers picked up and escorted the *Adriatic* of the White Star Line. As may be imagined, the Americans on board were delighted to see a destroyer with an American flag darting about the great vessel like a porpoise, while the British appreciated to the full the significance of the occasion—so much so that the following message was formulated and wirelessed to the destroyer:

"British passengers on board a steamship bound for a British port under the protection of an American torpedo-boat destroyer send their hearty greetings to her commander and her officers and crew and desire to express their keen appreciation of this practical co-operation between the government and people of the United States and the British Empire who are now fighting together for the freedom of the seas."

One may imagine with what emotions the officers and men of the American war-ship, bound for duty in enemy seas and at the very outset having a great greyhound intrusted to their care, received this glowing despatch.

There were many functions attending the arrival of the Americans at Queenstown, aside from those already set forth. Many of the seamen were granted shore-leave and were immediately captured by the townspeople, who took them to their homes and entertained most lavishly. They were the first American naval men that the Queenstowners had seen at close quarters in years, and the bluejackets were bombarded with questions.

And while the jackies were thus being treated the American officers made a memorable visit to Cork. They journeyed up the River Lee in an admiral's barge accompanied by Captain Evans. At the Cork custom-house they were met by distinguished military officers, by the lord-lieutenant of the county, and by the lord mayor of Cork. It was a most memorable occasion, and when they returned they found the British and American seamen on such good terms that the two bodies had already tried each other out in friendly fisticuffs, the net results being common respect one for the other.

Announcement of the arrival of the American vessels was made by the British Admiralty, the American Navy Department, with a modest reticence which ever since has been characteristic, saying nothing until the time came to confirm the admiralty's statement. In doing this Secretary Daniels announced that as a matter of fact an American flotilla of destroyers had arrived at an English port on May 4, and the vessels thereof engaged in the work of submarine hunting in both the Atlantic and in co-operation with the French in the Mediterranean. About the same time it was stated that a body of naval aviators, the first American fighting-men to serve from the shore, had been landed in England.

Soon after this announcement came another from Washington, giving an interchange of wireless amenities between Vice-Admiral Sir David Beatty, commander of the British Grand Fleet, to Rear-Admiral Henry T. Mayo, commanding the United States Atlantic Fleet:

"The Grand Fleet rejoices that the Atlantic Fleet will share in preserving the liberties of the world and maintaining the chivalry of the sea."

And Admiral Mayo's reply:

"The United States Atlantic Fleet appreciates the message from the British Fleet, and welcomes opportunities for work with the British Fleet for the freedom of the seas."

REDUCED LOSSES

In confirming the British announcement of the arrival of the flotilla at Queenstown, Secretary Daniels said:

"It has been the purpose of the United States Navy to give the largest measure of assistance to other countries at war with Germany that is consistent with the full and complete protection of our own coast and territorial waters."

Within a week after the arrival of our flotilla at Queenstown, the vessels thereof ranging the seas side by side with the British, submarine losses showed a marked reduction, and it was even more marked the second week of our co-operation. It was also stated that more submarines had been sunk in the week of May 12 than in the previous month.

In preparing for co-operation with the British destroyers, the American officers received lectures on the subject of effective submarine fighting, while depth-bombs and appliances for releasing them were supplied to the American boats, and all surplus gear and appurtenances of various sorts were taken from the American vessels and stored ashore.

It was noted as a curious fact that the United

States Navy had really been a warm-weather navy. The ships were sent south in winter for drills and target practice, usually in Guantanamo Bay; in the spring they engaged in manœuvres off the Virginia Capes, and in summer went to Newport, Provincetown, and other New England points. Again, life in a destroyer on the wintry Atlantic was not the most comfortable life in the world. There were cold fogs, icy winds and fearful storms in the war zone, and the thin steel hulls of the destroyers offered little in the way of creature comforts. This fact perhaps gave color to the report from Queenstown that our men were prepared in every respect save that of clothing, a statement that was indignantly refuted by the Navy Department, and a list of the garments furnished the sailors was submitted. It was an adequate list and quite effectually silenced further rumors on that score. As a matter of fact, no complaint ever came from the jackies themselves. They had sea-boots, pea-jackets, short, heavy double-breasted overcoats, knitted watch-caps, heavy woollen socks, jerseys, extra jackets of lambskin wool, oil-skins, and navy

AN UNGALLANT POET

uniform suits—a complete outfit surely. In the meantime the young women, elderly women, too, of the country were busily engaged in knitting helmets, sweaters, mittens, and the like. Some of the girls, more romantic than others, inserted their names and addresses in the articles they sent to the sailors. Here is a little *jeu d'esprit* that one girl received from a sailor of Admiral Sims's command:

> "Some sox; some fit!
> I used one for a helmet.
> And one for a mitt.
> I hope I shall meet you
> When I've done my bit.
> But who in the devil
> Taught you to knit?"

The reader may be sure that other, many other, more appreciative messages were sent to the devoted young women of the country, and that in many cases interesting correspondence was opened.

On May 25, 1917, Admiral Sims cabled to Secretary Daniels that Berlin knew of American plans for sending our destroyers to Europe four days before the vessels arrived at Queenstown, and that twelve mines had been placed across the entrance to the harbor the day before the destroyer flotilla reached their destination. The activity of British mine-sweepers prevented whatever might have occurred. This gave rise to considerable discussion in this country as to German spies here, and as an instance of their work in keeping in touch with naval affairs the following story was told in naval circles: When the oil-ship *Vacuum*, with Lieutenant Thomas and a naval gun crew on board, sailed from this country, the captain had instructions where to pick up British destroyers at a certain point off the Irish coast. The *Vacuum* arrived at the designated spot, and before the war-ships arrived a submarine appeared out of the water.

"I see," said the German commander, appearing out of the conning-tower, "that you kept your appointment."

And then the *Vacuum* was sent to the bottom. Later, under the convoy system, submarines began to be very wary in the matter of triumphant conversations with officers of merchantmen. In fact, this appears to have been the last interchange of the sort.

WORK OF DESTROYERS

Working with the British, the American destroyers patrolled the seas six days at a stretch, each craft being assigned to a certain area, as far out as three hundred miles off shore. Returning to port, the destroyers would lie at their moorings two and three days. Later the time in port was reduced. But it depended upon conditions. The orders to the Americans were: first, destroy submarines; second, escort and convoy merchant ships; third, save lives. And in all three respects the Americans from the very outset have so conducted themselves and their craft as to earn the highest encomiums from the Entente admiralties.

The Americans entered very heartily into their work, and developed ideas of their own, some of which the British were very glad to adopt. Between the men of the two navies there has been the best sort of feeling.

CHAPTER V

BRITISH AND AMERICAN DESTROYERS OPERATING HAND IN HAND—ARRIVAL OF NAVAL COLLIER "JUPITER"—SUCCESSFUL TRIP OF TRANSPORTS BEARING UNITED STATES SOLDIERS CONVOYED BY NAVAL VESSELS—ATTACK ON TRANSPORTS WARDED OFF BY DESTROYERS—SECRETARY BAKER THANKS SECRETARY DANIELS—VISIT TO OUR DESTROYER BASE—ATTITUDE OF OFFICERS TOWARD MEN — GENESIS OF THE SUBMARINE — THE CONFEDERATE SUBMARINE "HUNLEY"

A CORRESPONDENT who visited the British base on the Irish coast a month after the arrival of the Americans, found the two fleets operating hand in hand and doing effective work. With the boats out four and five, and then in port coaling and loading supplies two and three days, the seamen were getting practically half a day shore-leave every week. The seamen endured the routine grind of patrol and convoy work, accepting it as the price to be paid for the occasional fights with submarines.

An assignment to convoy a liner from home is regarded as a choice morsel, and the boats that get the job are looked upon as favored

ADMIRAL SIMS APPRECIATED

craft. The transatlantic passengers invariably make a fuss over the Americans, and the interchange of amenities gives our sailors concrete evidence of how their work is regarded in this country.

On June 6, 1917, Secretary Daniels, with warrantable pride, announced the arrival in a French port of the naval collier *Jupiter*, with 10,500 tons of wheat and other supplies. The *Jupiter* is nearly as large as a battleship, and stands out of the water like a church. Nevertheless, the collier, completely armed and well able to take care of herself, made the trip without convoy. She was the first electrically propelled vessel of large size ever built, and her performance was so good that it led to the adoption of the electric drive for all our new battleships and cruisers.

In the meantime, with our destroyers working valiantly in the fight against the submarines, Admiral Sims, their commander, had made himself indispensable to the British Admiralty, whose high regard was manifested on June 19, when, as already noted, he was appointed to take charge of operations of the Allied naval forces in Irish waters while the British commander-in-chief was absent for a short period. Washington had given wide powers to Admiral Sims to the end that he might be in a position to meet any emergency that might arise. While much of his time was spent in Paris and London, his home was at the Irish base, a fine old mansion 300 feet above the town, with beautiful lawns and gardens, having been turned over to him.

In June of 1917, June 4, it was announced in Washington that an American squadron had arrived in South American waters in accordance with the plan of relieving British and French cruisers of patrol duty in waters of the western hemisphere, merely one more instance of the scope of the plans which the Navy Department had formulated when we entered the war.

On June 25 came word that the first American convoy (transports with American troops), under direction of Rear-Admiral Albert M. Gleaves, commander of our convoy system, had arrived safely at a port in France. On July 3 the last units of ships with supplies and horses reached its destination. The expedition was divided into contingents, each contingent including troop-ships and an escort of sea-fighters. An ocean rendezvous with American destroyers operating in European waters was arranged, and carried out in minutest detail.

The convoy did not cross the seas without incident. In the newspapers of July 4 the country was electrified by a statement issued by the Creel bureau of a rather thrilling combat between war-ships attached to the convoy and German submarines, in which the U-boat was badly worsted. Details were given, and all in all the whole affair as presented was calculated to give the utmost unction to American pride. Next day, however, came a despatch from the American flotilla base in British waters which set forth that the story of the attack as published in the United States was inaccurate. There was no submarine attack, said the report, and no submarine was seen. One destroyer did drop a depth-bomb, but this was merely by way of precaution. Quite a stir followed, and it was not until Secretary Daniels some time later published facts as set forth in a cipher message from Admiral Gleaves that the country realized that, while the original account was somewhat overdrawn, there was substantial ground for the belief that several transports had had narrow escapes. To a correspondent who was on one of the transports we are indebted for the following narrative of the attack:

"It was past midnight. The flotilla was sweeping through a calm sea miles from the point of debarkation, and tense nerves were beginning to relax. The sky was cloudy and the moon obscured, but the phosphorescence of water common in these latitudes at this season marked the prow and wake of the advancing ships with lines of smoky flame. It was this, perhaps, that saved us from disaster—this and the keenness of American eyes, and the straightness of American shooting. From the high-flung superstructure of a big ship one of the eager lookouts noted an unwonted line of shining foam on the port bow. In a second he realized that here at last was the reality of peril. It could be nothing else than the periscope of a submarine. The Germans were not less swift

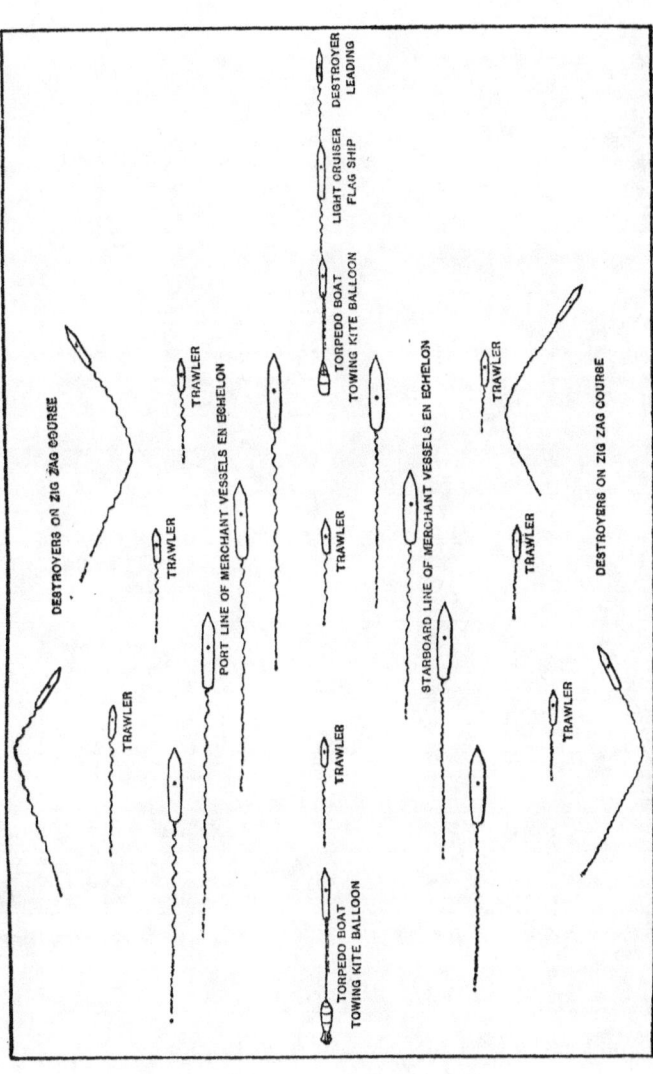

Position of ships in a convoy.

IN ACTION

in action. Almost at the moment that the alarm was given a gleaming line of bubbles, scarcely twenty feet from the bow of one of the transports wherein thousands were sleeping, announced the torpedo with its fatal burden of explosive. Then 'hell broke loose.' Firing every gun available, the big ship swung on a wide circle out of line to the left. A smaller war-ship slipped into the place of the big fighter, driving shells into the sea. Whether any landed or not may not be said. The Germans fired three, if not four, torpedoes. It was God's mercy that they all went astray among so many of our ships. The whole business lasted only a minute and a half. I know, because one of those Easterners from somewhere up in Maine coolly timed the mix-up with his stop-watch. But believe me, it added more than that time to my life. The second attack occurred next morning. Every living soul on the transports had been thrilled by the news of the night's events, and from early hours the decks were lined with amateur lookouts. The morning was fine, and a light breeze rippled up wavelets that twinkled in the sunlight. Suddenly about 10.30

o'clock there came a wild yell from one of the leading transports. Though the jackies affect to dispute it, I was assured that it was from a far-sighted youngster from Arizona, who first descried and then announced the deadly line of bubbles. No periscope was visible this time, and for the first moment those on the bridges of the destroyers were incredulous. Then the unmistakable bubble lines clean across the bows put the certainty of danger beyond question. Once again fortune favored us. The submarine was in front instead of in the deadliest position on the flank toward the rear. Perhaps the U-boat commander was rattled by the magnitude of his opportunity. Perhaps one of his excited pirates let go too soon. Anyway, it is agreed by experts that he would have been far more dangerous had he waited unseen until part of the flotilla at least had passed beyond him.

"Dearly did the Germans pay for their error. Like a striking rattlesnake, one of our destroyers darted between a couple of transports. Her nose was so deep in the sea as to be almost buried, while a great wave at the stern threw

ONE MORE "SUB" GONE

a shower of spray on the soldiers massed at the transport's bow. That destroyer ran right along the line of bubbles like a hound following a trail, and when it came to the spot where the commander estimated the submarine must be lurking, he released a depth-bomb. A column of smoke and foam rose fifty feet in the air, and the destroyer herself rose half out of the water under the shock of the explosion. It is said that in the midst of the column of water were seen fragments of steel and wood, and oil also was reported on the water. This meant that at least one submarine had paid the supreme price for the spread of kultur on the high seas."

As in all thrilling incidents of the sort, there was a note of comedy. It was supplied by a negro roustabout on one of the large transports. This darky throughout the trip had been very fearful of submarines, and when the actual moment of danger came he acted upon a predetermined course, and shinned up the mainmast as though Old Nick himself were at his heels. When the excitement was over an officer called up to him:

"Hello, up there; come down. It's all over."

"Me come down," came the voice from on high. "Mistah officah, I ain't nevah gwine to come down; no suh. De place fo man is on de dry land, yas suh. Ocean wa'nt nevah made for man; de ocean's fo fishes, dat's all. I'm gwine to stay up heah until I see de land. Den I'se gwine to jump."

History fails to record how long he remained in his retreat. Probably until he became hungry.

This, then, appears to be what happened to our first convoy. That there was an attack upon the convoy by submarines in force, as set forth in the original statement from Washington, now seems altogether unlikely, and whether our destroyers sunk one or more of the undersea assailants is a matter of opinion. It does, however, seem likely that the one waging the second attack was accounted for.

The War Department was not slow to recognize the effectiveness with which our navy had transported the first oversea expedition to France as the following message from Secretary of War Newton D. Baker to Secretary Daniels will show.

"War Department,
"Washington, July 3.

"Word has just come to the War Department that the last ships conveying Gen. Pershing's expeditionary force arrived safely to-day. As you know, the Navy Department assumed the responsibility for the safety of these ships on the sea and through the danger zone. The ships themselves and their convoys were in the hands of the navy, and now that they have arrived and carried without the loss of a man our soldiers who are first to represent America in the battle for Democracy, I beg leave to tender to you, to the admiral, and to the navy the hearty thanks of the War Department and of the army. This splendid achievement is an auspicious beginning, and it has been characterized throughout by the most cordial and effective co-operation between the two military services.

"Cordially yours,
"NEWTON D. BAKER."

In the meantime Americans living in England had organized to do everything in their power to make the lives of the seamen of the destroyer fleet comfortable. Plans were at once formulated and work begun on a club, the United States Naval Men's Club at the American base. This club, which is now completed, contains dormitories, shower-baths, a canteen, and a billiard room with two pool-tables. There is an auditorium for moving-picture shows and other entertainments, reading-rooms, and in fact everything that would tend to make the men feel at home and divert their leisure hours.

A correspondent for the Associated Press, who visited the club when it was completed, has testified to its great attractiveness, and from his pen also has come the most effective description of our destroyers as they return to their base from duty in the North Sea. One destroyer which he inspected had had the good fortune to be able to bring back the crews of two torpedoed merchantmen. The mariners were picked up on the fourth day out, and had the unique experience of joining in a lookout for their undoers before the destroyer returned to its base. Despite her battles with heavy seas and high winds, the destroyer was as fit as any of her sister craft lying at anchor near by. Her brasswork glistened in the sunshine, and her decks were as clean as a good housewife's kitchen. The crew, a majority of them mere boys, were going about their work with every manifestation of contentment.

"They are," observed the commander, "the most alert sailors in the world." The destroyer carried five 4-inch guns, the type most used on destroyers. Ten feet behind the guns were cases of shells, each shell weighing sixty pounds. When firing upon a submarine the shells are passed by hand to the gunners—no small task when the sea is heavy. At the gun the gunner is equipped with a head-gear, like that worn by telephone girls, through which he receives sighting directions from the officer on the bridge. Speaking-tubes also convey messages from the bridge to the gunners.

These "voice-tubes," as they are called, run to all the guns, but take the most circuitous routes, running way below deck in order that damage by shell-fire to the upper part of the vessel might not affect communication from the bridge to the gunners. On different parts of the deck were three canvas-covered boxes, each containing six loaded rifles, eighteen in all. These were for use against boarding-parties.

The vessel also contained numerous torpedo-tubes, always loaded. The destroyer registered about a thousand tons, and carried a crew of ninety-five men, who were reported as "a great happy family." The commanding officer said that there was surprisingly little homesickness among the men, many of whom had never before been so far from their native land.

"We invite questions and suggestions from our men," said one of the officers to the correspondent. "We want them to feel that no one is ever too old to learn."

The seamen sleep on berths suspended from the steel walls of the destroyers, berths which, when not in use, can be closed very much after the manner of a folding bed. When "submarined" crews are rescued the sailors willingly give up their comfortable berths and do everything else in their power to make the shipwrecked mariners comfortable. The men receive their mail from home uncensored. It arrives about every ten days in bags sealed in

A GREAT GAME 109

the United States. Their own letters, however, are censored, not only by an officer aboard ship, but by a British censor. However, there has been little or no complaint by the men on the ground of being unable to say what they wish to their loved ones.

"The men," wrote an officer recently, "look upon submarine-hunting as a great game. The only time they are discontented is when a situation which looks like an approaching fight resolves itself into nothing. The seas of the war zone are, of course, filled with all sorts of flotsam and jetsam, and very often that which appears to be a periscope is nothing of the sort. But when a real one comes—then the men accept it as a reward."

In view of all that has been said thus far and remains to be said concerning the submarine, it might be well to digress for a moment and devote the remainder of this chapter to a consideration of the undersea fighter, its genesis, what it now is, and what it has accomplished. We all know that the submarine was given to the world by an American inventor—that is to say, the submarine in very much the form that we know it to-day, the effective, practical submarine. The writer recalls witnessing experiments more than twenty years ago on the Holland submarine—the first modern submarine type—and he recalls how closely it was guarded in the early days of 1898, when it lay at Elizabethport and the Spanish war-ship *Viscaya*, Captain Eulate, lay in our harbor. This was a month or so after the destruction of the battleship *Maine* in Havana Harbor, and threats against the Spanish had led, among other precautions, to an armed guard about the *Holland* lest some excitable person take her out and do damage to the *Viscaya*. There was no real danger, of course, that this would happen; it merely tends to show the state of public mind.

Well, in any event, the *Holland*, and improved undersea craft subsequently developed, converted the seemingly impossible into the actual. To an Englishman, William Bourne, a seaman-gunner must be credited the first concrete exposition of the possibilities of an undersea fighter. His book, "Inventions or Devices,"

ORIGINAL SUBMARINE

published in 1578, contains a comprehensive description of the essential characteristics of the undersea boat as they are applied to-day. From the days of the sixteenth century on down through the years to the present time, submarine construction and navigation have passed through various stages of development. Captain Thomas A. Kearney, U. S. N., in an interesting monograph published through the United States Naval Institute at Annapolis, says that of the early American inventors, particular mention should be made of the work of David Bushnell and Robert Fulton, both of whom have been termed the "father of the submarine." Bushnell's boat, completed in 1775–6, was much in advance of anything in its class at the time. The boat, which was, of course, water-tight, was sufficiently commodious to contain the operator and a sufficient amount of air to support him for thirty minutes. Water was admitted into a tank for the purpose of descending and two brass force-pumps ejected the water when the operator wished to rise. Propulsion was by an oar astern, working as the propeller of a vessel works to-day. Practically Bushnell in one attempt to destroy a British war-ship in the Hudson River was able to get under the British frigate *Eagle* without detection, but was unable to attach the mine which the boat carried.

Fulton's inventive genius directed toward a submarine took tangible shape in 1800 when the French Government built the *Nautilus* in accordance with his plans. Both France and the United States carried on experimental work with Fulton's designs, under his personal supervision, but there is no record of any marked achievement.

The first submarine within the memory of men living to-day, the first practical, albeit crude, undersea boat, was the *H. L. Hunley*, built at Mobile, Ala., under the auspices of the Confederate Navy and brought from that port to Charleston on flat cars for the purpose of trying to break the blockade of that port by Federal war-ships. The *Hunley* was about forty feet long, six in diameter, and shaped like a cigar. Its motive power came from seven men turning cranks attached to the propeller-shaft. When working their hardest these men

THE *HUNLEY*

could drive the boat at a speed of about four miles an hour.

Several attempts to use the *Hunley* were unsuccessful, each time it sank, drowning its crew of from eight to ten men. These experiments, which were carried on in shallow water at Charleston, mark one of the bright pages in our seafaring annals, as crew after crew went into the boat facing practically certain death to the end that the craft might be made effective. Each time the vessel sank she was raised, the dead crew taken out, and a new experiment with a new crew made. In all thirty-three men were sacrificed before it was finally decided that the boat could make her way out to the blockading line. It was on the night of February 17, 1864, that the *Hunley* set out on her last journey. The vessel submerged, reached the side of the United States steamship *Housatonic*, and successfully exploded a mine against the hull of the Federal war-ship, sending her to the bottom.

But in the explosion the submersible herself was sunk and all on board were lost. The commander of the expedition was Lieutenant

George E. Dixon, of Alabama, who with his crew well appreciated their danger. It is supposed that the *Hunley* was drawn down in the suction of the sinking war-ship; she could not arise from the vortex, and that was the last of her and of her brave crew. The North was tremendously excited over the incident and the South elated, but no other ship was attacked from beneath the water in the course of the war.

Holland's boat, built in 1877, was the first to use a gas-engine as a propulsive medium, but it was not until the final adoption of the gas-engine for surface work, followed later by the internal-combustion gasolene-engine and the use of electric storage-battery for subsurface work, as well as the invention of the periscope and various other devices, that the submarine was developed to a present state of effectiveness, which sees it crossing the Atlantic from Germany, operating off our shores and returning to Germany without being obliged to put into port; which, also, sees it capable of navigating under water at a speed of from seven to nine knots, with torpedoes ready for use in the tubes and guns of effective caliber mounted on deck. It has, indeed, been asserted that the airplane and the submarine have relegated the battleship to the limbo of desuetude; but as to that the continued control of the seas by Great Britain with her immense battle-fleet, supplemented by our tremendous engines of war, certainly argues for no such theory. What the future may bring forth in the way of submarines, armored and of great size, no man may say. But at present the submarine, while tremendously effective, has not done away with the battleship as a mighty element in the theory of sea power.

As to life on a submersible, let us construct from material which has come to us from various sources in the past three years a little story which will give a better knowledge of the workings of the German undersea boat than many pages of technical description would do. An undertaking of the sort will be the more valuable because we of the Allies are inclined to consider the submarine problem only in relation to our side of the case, whereas the fact is that the submarine operates under great difficulties and dangers, and in an ever-increasing degree leaves port never to be heard from again. We may, then, begin the following chapter with a scene in Kiel, Zeebrugge, or any German submarine base.

CHAPTER VI

ON A GERMAN SUBMARINE—FIGHT WITH A DESTROYER—PERISCOPE HIT—RECORD OF THE SUBMARINE IN THIS WAR—DAWNING FAILURE OF THE UNDERSEA BOAT—FIGURES ISSUED BY THE BRITISH ADMIRALTY—PROOF OF DECLINE—OUR NAVY'S PART IN THIS ACHIEVEMENT

A FIRST lieutenant with acting rank of commander takes the order in the gray dawn of a February day. The hulk of an old corvette with the Iron Cross of 1870 on her stubby foremast is his quarters in port, and on the corvette's deck he is presently saluted by his first engineer and the officer of the watch. On the pier the crew of the U-47½ await him. At their feet the narrow gray submarine lies alongside, straining a little at her cables.

"Well, we've got our orders at last," begins the commander, addressing his crew of thirty, and the crew look solemn. For this is the U-47½'s first experience of active service. She has done nothing save trial trips hitherto and has just been overhauled for her first fighting cruise. Her commander snaps out a number of orders. Provisions are to be taken "up to the neck." Fresh water is to be put aboard, and engine-room supplies to be supplemented.

A mere plank is the gangway to the little vessel. As the commander, followed by his officers, comes aboard, a sailor hands to each of the officers a ball of cotton waste, the one article aboard a submarine which never leaves an officer's hands. For of all oily, grimy, greasy places the inside of the submarine is supreme. The steel walls, the doors, the companion-ladders all sweat oil, and the hands must be wiped dry at every touch. Through a narrow hole aft the commander descends by a straight iron ladder into a misty region whose only light comes from electric glow-lamps. The air reeks with the smell of oil. Here is the engine-room and, stifling as the atmosphere is with the hatches up, it is as nothing compared to what the men have to breathe when everything is hermetically sealed.

Here are slung hammocks, where men of one engine-watch sleep while their comrades move about the humming, purring apartment, bumping the sleepers with their heads and elbows.

But little things like that do not make for wakefulness on a submarine. The apartment or vault is about ten feet long; standing in the middle, a man by stretching out his arms may easily have his fingers in contact with the steel walls on either side. Overhead is a network of wires, while all about there is a maze of levers, throttles, wheels, and various mechanical appliances that are the dismay of all but the mind specially trained in submarine operation.

The commander very minutely inspects everything; a flaw will mean a long sleep on the bottom, thirty men dead. Everything is tested. Then, satisfied, the commander creeps through a hole into the central control-station, where the chief engineer is at his post. The engineer is an extraordinary individual; the life of the boat and its effectiveness are in his care. There must be lightning repairs when anything goes wrong on an undersea craft, and in all respects the chief's touch must be that of a magician.

Exchanging a word or two with the chief engineer, the commander continues his way to the torpedo-chamber where the deadly "silverfish," as the Germans have named the hideous projectiles, lie. Perhaps he may stroke their gleaming backs lovingly; one may not account for the loves of a submarine commander. The second-in-command, in charge of the armament, joins him in the torpedo-room and receives final instructions regarding the torpedo and the stowing of other explosives. Forward is another narrow steel chamber, and next to it is a place like a cupboard where the cook has just room to stand in front of his doll's-house galley-stove. It is an electric cooker, of course. Housewives who operate kitchenettes in Manhattan will appreciate the amount of room which the cook has. And, by the way, this being a German submarine, the oily odors, the smell of grease, and the like are complicated by an all-pervading smell of cabbage and coffee. Two little cabins, the size of a clothes-chest, accommodate the deck and engine-rooms officers—two in each. Then there is a little box-cabin for the commander.

As the sun rises higher the commander goes into his cabin and soon after emerges on deck. His coat and trousers are of black leather lined with wool, a protection against oil, cold, and wet weather. The crew are at their stations.

"Machines clear," comes a voice from the control-station.

"Clear ship," comes the order from the bridge, followed by "Cast off."

The cables hiss through the water and slap on the landing-stage; the sound of purring fills the submarine which glides slowly into open water. Into the bay comes another U-boat. Stories of her feat in sinking a steamship loaded with mutton for England has preceded her. There has been loss of life connected with that sinking, but this makes no difference to the Teutonic mind, and the officer of the U-47½ shouts his congratulations.

Now the submarine is out in the open sea, the waves are heavy and the vessel rolls uncomfortably. The craft, it may be remarked, is not the craft for a pleasant sea-voyage. The two officers hanging onto the rails turn their eyes seaward. The weather increases in severity. The officers are lashed to the bridge. There they must stay; while the boat plies the surface the bridge must not be left by the commander and his assistant. Sometimes they remain thus on duty two and three days. Food is carried to them and they eat it as they stand.

It may be that the commander is trying to balance a plate of heavy German soup in his hand as a cry comes from a lookout.

"Smoke on the horizon, off the port bow, sir."

The commander withdraws from his food, shouts an order and an electric alarm sounds inside the hull. The ship buzzes with activity. The guns on deck are hastily housed. Bridge appurtenances are housed also, and sailors dive down through the deck-holes. The commander follows. Water begins to gurgle into the ballast-tanks while the crew seal every opening. Down goes the U-47½ until only her periscope shows, a periscope painted sea-green and white —camouflaged. The eyes of the watch-officer are glued to the periscope.

"She is a Dutchman, sir," he says at length. The commander steps to the periscope and takes a look. The Dutchman has no wireless and is bound for some continental port. It is not wise to sink every Dutch boat one meets—although German submarines have sunk a sufficient number of them, in all conscience. At all events, the steamship goes in peace and the submarine comes to the surface. The commander is glad, because electric power must be used when the vessel is moving under water and there must be no waste of this essential element.

So the submarine proceeds on her way, wallowing and tumbling through the heavy graybacks of the North Sea. At length after fifty-four hours the necessity of sleep becomes apparent. The ballast-tanks are filled and the craft slowly descends to the sandy bottom of the sea. It is desirable that the crew go to sleep as quickly as possible, because when men are asleep they use less of the priceless supply of oxygen which is consumed when the boat is under water. However, the commander allows the men from half an hour to an hour for music and singing. The phonograph is turned on and there on the bottom of the North Sea the latest songs of Berlin are ground out while the crew sit about, perhaps joining in the choruses— they sang more in the early days of the war than they do to-day—while the officers sit around their mess-table and indulge in a few social words before they retire.

In the morning water from the tanks is expelled and the boat rises to greet a smiling sea. Also to greet a grim destroyer. The war-ship sees her as she comes up from a distance of perhaps a mile away. All steam is crowded on while the leaden-gray fighter—the one craft that the submarine fears—makes for her prey. Sharp orders ring through the U-boat. The tanks are again filled, and while the commander storms and ejaculates, everything is made tight and the vessel sinks beneath the surface. The electric-motors are started and the submarine proceeds under water in a direction previously determined, reckoned in relation to the course of the approaching destroyer.

Presently comes a dull explosion. The destroyer arriving over the spot where the undersea boat was last seen, has dropped a depth-bomb, which has exploded under the surface at a predetermined depth. The submarine commander grins. The bomb was too far away to do damage, although the craft has trembled under the shock. There comes another shock, this time not so palpable. Eventually all is quiet.

For an hour the submarine proceeds blindly under water, and then cautiously her periscope is thrust above the surface. Nothing in sight. Orders sound through the vessel and she rises to the surface. She could have remained below, running under full headway, for six hours before coming to the surface. So the day goes on. Toward nightfall smoke again is seen on the horizon. It proves to be a large freighter ladened, apparently, with cattle. Two destroyers are frisking about her, crossing her bow, cutting around her stern. The steamship herself is zigzagging, rendering accurate calculations as to her course uncertain.

By this time, of course, the submarine has submerged. The watch-officer and the commander stand by the periscope, watching the approaching craft. The periscope may not be left up too long; the watchers on the destroyers and on the deck of the vessel, which is armed, are likely to spy it at any time. So the periscope is alternately run down and run up. The submarine has moved so that the steamship will pass her so as to present a broadside. Up comes the periscope for one last look. The observer sees a puff of smoke from the deck of a destroyer and a quick splash of water obscures the view momentarily.

"They have seen us and are firing."

But the steamship is now within a mile, within fairly accurate torpedo range. An order rolls into the torpedo-room and the crew prepare for firing. In the meantime a shower of shells explode about the periscope. There comes a sudden vagueness on the glass into which the observer has been gazing.

"The periscope has been hit."

Thoughts of launching the torpedo vanish. Safety first is now the dominant emotion. Additional water flows into the tanks and the craft begins to settle. But as she does so there is a sudden flood of water into the control-room; a hoarse cry goes up from the crew. The officers draw their revolvers. Evidently the injured periscope has caused a leak. Before anything can be done there is a tremendous grinding, rending explosion; the thin steel walls

BOMB DOES ITS WORK 127

contract under the force of the released energy. Above them the destroyer crew gazing eagerly at the geyser-like volume of water arising from the sea descry pieces of metal, dark objects of all sorts. The sea quiets and up from the depths arise clouds of oil, spreading slowly over the waves. The U-47½ has joined many a nobler craft upon the wastes of subaqueous depths.

But not always has the outcome of a submarine attack been so fortunate for us. There have been thousands of instances—many more of them in the past than at present, fortunately —where the U-boat returned to her base with a murderous story to tell. While it is certain that when the totals for the present year are compiled an engaging tale of reduced submarine effectiveness will be told; yet—as the British Government has announced—any effort to minimize what the submarine has done would work chiefly toward the slowing up of our ship-building and other activities designed to combat directly and indirectly the lethal activities of the submarine. And from a naval standpoint it is also essential that the effectiveness of the undersea craft be fully understood.

It was on January 31, 1917, that the German Government suddenly cast aside its peace overtures and astonished the world by presenting to the United States Government a note to the effect that from February 1 sea traffic would be stopped with every available weapon and without further notice in certain specified zones. The decree applied to both enemy and neutral vessels, although the United States was to be permitted to sail one steamship a week in each direction, using Falmouth as the port of arrival and departure. On February 3 President Wilson appeared before Congress and announced that he had severed diplomatic relations with Germany on the ground that the imperial government had deliberately withdrawn its solemn assurances in regard to its method of conducting warfare against merchant vessels. Two months later, April 6, as already noted, Congress declared that a state of war with Germany existed.

The German people were led to believe that an aggregate of 1,000,000 tons of shipping would be destroyed each month and that the wastage would bring England to her knees in six months and lead to peace. The six months went by, but the promises of the German Government were not fulfilled. Instead the submarine war brought the United States into the struggle and this, in the words of Philipp Scheidemann, leader of the German majority Socialists, has been "the most noticeable result."

None the less, the submarine, used ruthlessly, without restrictions, proved itself to be an unrivalled weapon of destruction, difficult to combat by reason of its ability to stalk and surprise its quarry, while remaining to all intents and purposes invisible. It has taken heavy toll of ships and men, and has caused privation among the peoples of the Entente nations; it is still unconquered, but month by month of the present year its destructiveness has been impaired until now there may be little doubt that the number of submarines destroyed every month exceeds the number of new submarines built, while the production of ship tonnage in England and the United States greatly outweighs the losses. In other words, the submarine, as an element in the settling of the war in a manner favorable to Germany, has steadily lost influence, and, while it is not now a negligible factor, it is, at least, a minor one and growing more so.

Secret figures of the British Admiralty on submarine losses and world ship-building issued in March, 1918, show that from the outbreak of war, in August, 1914, to the end of 1917, the loss was 11,827,080 tons. Adding the losses up to April of the present year—when the submarine sinkings began to show a markedly decreased ratio—and we get a total of 13,252,692 tons. The world's tonnage construction in the four years 1914-17 was 6,809,080 tons. The new construction in England and the United States for the first quarter of 1918 was 687,221 tons, giving a total from the beginning of the war to April 1 of 1918, 7,750,000 tons built outside of the Central Powers since the beginning of the war, with a final deficit of about 5,500,000 tons. Of this deficit the year 1917 alone accounted for 3,716,000 tons.

From the last quarter of 1917, however, the margin between construction and loss has been narrowing steadily. In the first quarter of 1918 the construction in Great Britain and America alone was over 687,000 tons and the

From a photograph copyright by Enrique Muller.

A U. S. submarine at full speed on the surface of the water.

losses for the whole world were 1,123,510 tons. Here is a deficit for three months—the first three months of the present year—of 436,000 tons, or an annual average of 1,750,000 tons, which is a deficit one-half less than that of the black year of 1917. When figures at the end of the present year are revealed we may find that we have reckoned too little upon the shipbuilding activity of both England and the United States, in which event the deficit may prove to be even less. But in any event the dry figures as set forth are worth perusal inasmuch as they point not only to the deadly effectiveness of the submarine in the first year of unrestricted activity, but show how valiantly the Allied sea power has dealt with a seemingly hopeless situation in the present year.

In the House of Commons not long ago a definite statement that the trend of the submarine war was favorable to the Allies was made. The one specific item given was that from January 1 to April 30, 1917, the number of unsuccessful attacks upon British steamships was 172, a weekly average of 10. Last year in the ten weeks from the end of February to the end of April there were 175 unsuccessful attacks, or a weekly average of 18. This statement was not exactly illuminating. For of itself a decline in the weekly number of unsuccessful attacks would imply an increase in the effectiveness of the U-boat—which we know is not so. What the House of Commons statement really meant, of course, was that the number of *successful* attacks had been declining as well as the number of unsuccessful attacks—or, in other words, that the German sea effort as a whole was declining. The U-boats are not hitting out as freely as they did a year ago. This argues that there are fewer of them than there were in 1917. For actual tonnage losses we have the word of the French Minister of Marine that the sinkings for April, 1918, were 268,000 tons, whereas in April of the previous year they were 800,000 tons, an appalling total.

"The most conclusive evidence we have seen of the failure of the enemy's submarine campaign is the huge American army now in France, and the hundreds of thousands of tons of stores brought across the Atlantic," said James Wilson, chairman of the American labor delegation, upon his return to England last May from a

PROGRESS OF U-BOAT FIGHT 133

visit to France and to the American army. "Less than twelve months have passed since General Pershing arrived in France with 50 men. The developments that have taken place since seem little short of miraculous.

Georges Leygues, Minister of Marine of France, in testifying before the Chamber of Deputies in May said that in November of 1917 losses through the submarine fell below 400,000 tons, and since has diminished continuously. He said that the number of submarines destroyed had increased progressively since January of the present year in such proportion that the effectiveness of enemy squadrons cannot be maintained at the minimum required by the German Government. The number of U-boats destroyed in January, February, and March was far greater in each month than the number constructed in those months. In February and April the number of submarines destroyed was three less than the total destroyed in the previous three months. These results, the minister declared, were due to the methodical character of the war against submarines, to the close co-ordination of the Allied navies; to the intrepidity and spirit animating the officers and crews of the naval and aerial squadrons, to the intensification of the use of old methods and to the employment of new ones.

We may lay to ourselves the unction that the reduced effectiveness of the submarine coincided with the entrance of our naval forces into the war. This is taking nothing from the French, British, and Italian navies; as a matter of truth, it would be gross injustice to ignore the fact that the large share of the great task has been handled through the immense resources of the British. But the coordinated effort which began with the arrival of our vessels on the other side, the utter freedom with which Secretary Daniels placed our resources at the service of the British was inspiring in its moral influences throughout the Entente nations, while practically there may be no doubt that our craft have played their fair share in the activities that have seen the steady decline of deadliness on the part of the U-boat. We may now consider the methods which our navy in collaboration with Allied sea power have employed in this combat for the freedom of the seas.

CHAPTER VII

HOW THE SUBMARINE IS BEING FOUGHT—DESTROYERS THE GREAT MENACE—BUT NETS, TOO, HAVE PLAYED THEIR PART—MANY OTHER DEVICES—GERMAN OFFICERS TELL OF EXPERIENCE ON A SUBMARINE CAUGHT IN A NET—CHASERS PLAY THEIR PART—THE DEPTH-BOMB—TRAWLER TRICKS—A CAMOUFLAGED SCHOONER WHICH TURNED OUT TO BE A TARTAR—AIRPLANES—GERMAN SUBMARINE MEN IN PLAYFUL MOOD

WHEN the submarines first began their attacks upon British war-ships and merchant vessels the admiralty was faced by a state of affairs which had been dealt with more or less in the abstract, the only practical lessons at hand being those of the Russo-Japanese War, which conflict, as a matter of fact, left rather an unbalanced showing so far as the undersea boat and the surface craft were concerned; in other words, the submersible had by all odds the advantage.

But England tackled the problem with bulldog energy, utilizing to that end not only her immense destroyer fleet, but a myriad of high-speed wooden boats, many of which were built in this country. They were called submarine-chasers, and while the destroyer and the seaplane, as one of the most effective weapons against the submarine, came to the fore, the chaser is employed in large numbers by England, France, and the United States.

The great usefulness of the destroyer lay not only in patrolling the seas in search of the U-boats, but of serving in convoys, protecting passenger and freight vessels, and in rescuing crews of vessels that had been sunk. There may be other methods of reducing Germany's sum total of submarines which are equally—if not more—effective than the destroyer; but, if so, we have not been made aware of that fact. Certain it is, however, that aside from the destroyer, steel nets, fake fishing and merchant sailing vessels, seaplanes and chasers have played their important part in the fight, while such a minor expedient as blinding the eye of the periscope by oil spread on the waters has not been without avail.

The United States Navy appears to have figured chiefly through its destroyer fleet. It has been stated that half the number of sailors who were in the navy when we entered the war

TRAINING SEAMEN

were sent to European waters. The system of training them involves a number of training-bases in Europe constantly filling up from American drafts. Each new destroyer that steams to Europe from our shores in due course sends back some of her men to form a nucleus for the crew of another new destroyer turning up in American waters. Their places are taken by drafts from the training-bases in Europe. The destroyer referred to as turning up in this country makes up her complement from the battleships and other naval units here. The training-bases in this country are established at Newport, Chicago, San Francisco, and Pelham Bay, N. Y. Here the men have many months' instruction. As their training approaches completion they are sent where needed, and thus the work of creating an immense army of trained seamen qualified for any sort of a task proceeds with mechanical precision.

Submarine hunting is very popular with our young jackies, and great is their satisfaction when some submarine falls victim to their vigilance, their courage, and their unerring eyes.

"But," said a young sea officer not long ago,

"the submarine is a difficult bird to catch. He holds the advantage over the surface craft. He always sees you first. Even when he is on the surface he is nearly awash, and when submerged only his periscope appears above the water. The submarine is not after animals of our breed—destroyers—and when he can he avoids them. We may go several weeks without putting an eye upon a single U-boat. When we do there is action, I can tell you. We start for him at full speed, opening up with all our guns in the hope of getting in a shot before he is able to submerge. But you may believe he doesn't take long to get below the surface. Anyway, the sub doesn't mind gun-fire much. They are afraid of depth charges—bombs which are regulated so that they will explode at any depth we wish. They contain two or three hundred pounds of high explosive, and all patrol vessels and destroyers carry them on deck and astern. When we see a submarine submerge we try to find his wake. Finding it, we run over it and drop a bomb. The explosion can be felt under water for a distance of several miles, but we have to get within ninety feet of the hull to damage it. This damage may or may not cause the undersea boat to sink. Inside of ninety feet, though, there isn't much doubt about the sinking.

"Patrol duty is a grind. The sea where we work is filled with wreckage for a distance of 300 miles off shore, and you can take almost any floating object for a periscope. Yes, we shoot at everything; ours is not a business in which to take chances. Convoy work is more interesting and more exciting than the round of patrol. The advantage of the convoy over the picking up and escorting of a merchantman by a patrol-boat is that in the convoy from six to ten destroyers can protect from ten to thirty merchantmen, while under the patrol system one destroyer watches one merchant craft. Convoy trips take our destroyers away from their base from six to eight days, and they are all trying days, especially so in dirty weather. On convoy duty no officer, and no man, has his clothes off from start to finish. Too many things may happen to warrant any sort of unpreparedness. Constant readiness is the watchword.

"At night difficulty and danger increase, chiefly because of the increased danger of collision. Collisions sometimes occur—what with the absence of lights, the zigzag course of the ships of the convoy, and the speed with which we travel. But as a rule the accidents are of the scraping variety, and all thus is usually well. The convoy is purely a defensive measure. The patrol is the offensive; in this the destroyers and other craft go out and look for the U-boats, the idea being to hound them out of the seas."

Then there are netting operations in which our sailors have played some part. The netting most often used is made of stout galvanized wire with a 15-foot mesh. This is cut into lengths of 170 feet, with a depth of 45 feet. On top of this great net are lashed immense blocks of wood for buoys. Two oil-burning destroyers take the netting, and hanging it between them as deep down in the water as it will go, are ready to seine the 'silverfish.' The range of a submarine's periscope is little over a mile in any sort of sea. Vessels that are belching clouds of smoke may be picked up at distances of from three to five miles, but no more. In other

NETTING OPERATIONS

words, watchful eyes gazing through binoculars may see a periscope as far as that periscope sees. The destroyers, bearing their net between them, then pick up a distant periscope. They chart the submarine's direction (this may be told by the direction in which the periscope is cutting the water) and calculate her speed. Then they steam to a point directly ahead of the submarine, and the lashings are cut away from the net. While it thus floats in the submarine's path the destroyers speed away out of eyeshot. In a large majority of cases it is claimed the submarine runs into that net, or one like it. Results are a probable disarrangement of her machinery and her balance upset. She may be thrown over on her back. If she comes up she goes down again for good and all with a hole shot in her hull; if not, it is just as well, a shell has been saved.

Submarines occasionally escape by changing their course after the nets have been set; but there appears to have been no instance of the destroyers themselves having been picked up by the periscope. This because they set pretty nearly as low as a submarine, and with their oil-burning propulsion give forth no telltale cloud of smoke. Other nets are hung from hollow glass balls, which the periscope cannot pick up against the sea water. These nets are set in profusion in the English Channel, the North Sea, or wherever submarines lurk, and they are tended just as the North River shad fishermen tend their nets. When a destroyer, making the rounds, sees that a glass ball has disappeared, there is more than presumptive evidence that something very valuable has been netted.

Naval Lieutenant Weddingen, of the German submarine U-17, has related the following experience with the British net system. The U-17 had left her base early in the morning and had passed into the North Sea, the boat being under water with periscope awash. "I looked through the periscope," said Weddingen, "and could see a red buoy behind my boat. When, ten minutes later, I looked I saw the buoy again, still at the same distance behind us. I steered to the right and then to the left, but the buoy kept on following us. I descended deeply into the water, but still saw the buoy floating on

NETTED! 143

the surface above us. At last I discovered that we had caught the chain of the buoy and that we were dragging it along with us.

"At the same time, also, I saw through the periscope that a strange small steamer was steering a course directly behind us and the buoy. At this time my sounding apparatus indicated that a screw steamer was in the vicinity. Observation revealed that five enemy torpedo-boats were approaching from the north. I increased the speed of the boat in the expectation of being able to attack one of them. The five torpedo-boats arranged themselves in a circle. I sank still deeper and got ready for eventualities.

"At this juncture my boat began to roll in a most incomprehensible manner. We began to rise and sink alternately. The steering-gear apparently was out of order. Soon afterward I discovered that we had encountered a wire netting and were hopelessly entangled in it. We had, in fact, got into the net of one of the hunters surrounding us.

"For an hour and a half the netting carried us with it, and although I made every effort to get clear of it, it seemed impossible. There was nothing to do but increase the weight in the submarine as much as possible so that I might try to break the netting. Fortunately, when we had started I had pumped in from five to six tons of water, filling all the tanks. I increased the weight of the boat to the utmost, and suddenly we felt a shock and were clear of the netting. I then descended as deeply in the water as I could, the monometer showing thirty metres. We remained under water for eighteen hours. When I wanted to ascertain where we were I noticed that my compass was out of order. For a time I steered by the green color of the water, but at last I had to get rid of the ballast in order to rise. I then discovered that the monometer continued to register the same depth, and was also out of order.

"I had, therefore, to be very careful not to rise too high and thus attract the attention of the torpedo-boats. Slowly the periscope rose above the surface, and I could see the enemy in front of me, and toward the left the east coast of England. I tried to turn to starboard, but the rudder did not work. In consequence, I had to sink again to the bottom of the sea, where I remained for six hours, at the end of which time I had succeeded in putting the compass in order, and also in repairing the steering-gear. But upon rising this time, we were detected by a torpedo-boat, which made straight for us, forcing me to descend again." (This apparently was before depth-bombs came into use.) "I remained submerged for two hours, then turned slowly outward, and at a distance of some fifty metres from the leading enemy craft, passed toward the open sea. At 9 o'clock in the evening we were able to rise and proceed in safety."

Here is a human document, is it not? It is the experience of the tarpon at the undersea end of the line, or, in human terms, the hidden drama of man against man, drama of the sort made possible by the ingenuity of this modern age.

Submarine-chasers are shallow craft, capable of a speed of thirty-five miles an hour or more, mounting guns fore and aft. Some of our chasers measure more than 200 feet over all (*Eagle* class), while others measure 110 feet.

The British, as already said, like the 80-footer, although using all sizes. Well, in any event, the chaser cruises about looking for surface waves. Now, the surface wave is the path marked by a submarine on the surface of the water. Even when she is fifty feet below the surface she leaves this palpable pathway up above. And few submarines travel at a depth of sixty feet. Then besides this track there are air-bubbles and spots of oil, all confirming the presence beneath the water of the U-boat.

So thereafter the chaser simply follows that surface wave until the submarine comes to the surface, as she must do sooner or later to get her bearings and look about for prey. When she does come up—she goes down for good. The hunt of the chaser has been aided in the past year or so by the depth-bomb, which did not exist in the first two and a half years of war. Equipped with this, she need not necessarily follow a surface wave all day; she simply drops the bomb down through this wave; at least she does under certain conditions.

This depth-bomb, by the way, is a wonderful invention, and with its perfection began the

From a photograph by Brown Brothers.

A submarine-chaser.

From a photograph by Brown Brothers.

A torpedo-destroyer.

THE DEPTH-BOMB

great decrease in submarine losses. The bomb is cylindrical and has in the top a well in which is fitted a small propeller. As the water comes in contact with the propeller the sinking motion causes it to revolve. As it revolves it screws down a detonator which comes in contact with the charge at ten, fifteen, twenty, or forty or more feet as designated by the hand of an indicator on the bomb. The hand of this indicator is, of course, set by the officer before the bomb is released either from a gun or from tracks along the deck.

Then there have been a number of tricks; some of them Yankee tricks, some of them the creatures of the equally fruitful British tar. One day in the North Sea a British patrol-vessel came across a trawler. It resembled the ordinary British trawler, but there were points of difference, points that interested the inquisitive —and suspicious—commander of the war-vessel. Chiefly there were a lot of stores upon her deck. She flew the Norwegian flag, and her skipper said he was neutral. But the British commander decided to take a chance. He arrested the crew, placed them in irons, and manned the trawler with a crew of French and English navy men.

The trawler hovered about in the same locality for three days, and then one morning, lo and behold, a periscope popped up close alongside. Seeing the waters clear of enemy ships, the U-boat came to the surface and frisked blithely up to the trawler. She was greeted by a shower of machine-gun bullets, and surrendered without ado. There was really nothing else for the surprised skipper to do. For when he had last seen that trawler she was the parent ship of the submarine flotilla operating in that vicinity. In all, before the week was over, that trawler had captured six submarines without the loss of a life, and no one injured.

Thereafter the parent-ship trawler was seized whenever the British could capture one, and the same expedient was tried. But after a time the Germans became wary of approaching parent-ships until they were convinced that their parenthood was more real than assumed.

Then one day after the Americans arrived a three-masted schooner was commandeered. They put a deck-load of lumber on her; at least

A FAKE SCHOONER 149

it was an apparent deck-load. It was really a mask for a broadside of 3-pounder guns, different sections of the deck-load swinging open to admit of free play of the guns, as levers were pulled.

The schooner, commanded by a Maine skipper and his crew, was turned loose in the North Sea. Astern towed a dingy; from the taffrail flew the American flag. Before long out popped a submarine. Aha! A lumber-laden vessel—American! The German commander, grinning broadly, stepped into a gig with a bombing crew; torpedoes were not wasted on sailing-vessels.

"Get into your dingy," he cried, motioning toward the craft dangling astern.

The Maine skipper, in his red underclothes, besought, and then cursed—while the German grinned the more broadly. Finally, however, the irate—sic—skipper and his crew of five clambered into their dingy as ordered by the commander of the submarine. And then! No sooner had the schooner crew cleared the windjammer than the deck-load of lumber resolved itself into a series of doors, and out of each door protruded a gun. It was the last of that submarine, of course. The schooner got five submarines before another submarine happened to witness the destruction of a companion craft.

Next day when the schooner approached a submarine the undersea boat let drive with a torpedo, and the joyous days of that particular wind-jammer were at an end. But thereafter the Germans seldom tried to bomb a sailing craft.

Airplanes have played their important part in the work of our navy in combating the submarine. Seaplanes are sent on patrol from regular bases or from the deck of a parent-vessel, a steamship of large size. Flying at a height of 10,000 feet, an airplane operator can see the shadow of a submarine proceeding beneath the surface. Thus viewing his prey, the aviator descends and drops a depth-bomb into the water. Our airmen have already won great commendation from the British Admiralty and aerial commanders. Whatever may have been the delays in airplane production in this country, the American Navy has not been at fault, and Secretary Daniels's young men went into British seaplanes when American planes were

AVIATORS IN ACTION 151

not at hand. From British Admiralty sources have come many tales of the skill and courage of the American aviators. There was one recent instance noted of an American pilot scouting for submarines who spotted a periscope. He dropped a bomb a few feet astern and a few feet ahead of that periscope, both bombs falling perfectly in line with the objective. He circled and then dropped a bomb in the centre of a disturbance in the water. Up came oil in great quantities.

Another American pilot managed the rare feat of dropping a bomb precisely upon the centre of the deck of a submarine, and had the unhappy experience of seeing it fail to explode —as recently happened in the submarine fight off Cape Cod, near Chatham.

In hunting for the submarines the American destroyers have patrolled an area as wide as that bounded roughly by the great V formed by New York, Detroit, and Knoxville, Tenn. And while patrolling they have become skilled in the use of the depth charges, in establishing smoke screens so as to hide vessels of a convoy from the periscope eye, and in marksmanship. One gun crew not long ago saw the spar of a sunken ship which they at first took to be a periscope. They shattered that spar at a distance of 2,000 yards—more than a mile.

Filled with the enthusiasm of each new encounter with the enemy, the Americans have not been slow to build upon their experience, devising more effective methods against the next affray. For example, two officers working on designs for new destroyers have introduced many new ideas gained from their experiences in submarine-hunting. Suggestions relating to improved gun-fire and the like are always arising from the men of the fleet, and often they are accepted and applied.

A new appliance—I don't know by whom invented—is an improved microphone, by which the revolutions of a propeller are not only heard, but the direction also is indicated, while the force of the under-water sound-waves are translated on an indicator in terms of proximity. The great drawback to this is that the submarines are also equipped with microphones of the sort—or at least are said to be.

It is usually a grim business on both sides;

but occasionally a bit of humor comes out of the seas. A case in point was the message received almost every night by an American destroyer in European waters. The radiogram said:

"My position is —— degrees north, and —— degrees west. Come and get me; I am waiting for you."

HANS ROSE.

Now Hans Rose was the name of the German submarine commander who visited Newport, October, 1917, as we have already narrated. Twice the destroyer proceeded swiftly to the location, but never did Hans Rose keep his appointment. If he had the American sailors would not have given Captain Rose's crew beer upon that occasion, as they did when Rose and his U-boat dropped into Newport harbor.

Then there is a submarine commander known throughout the American flotilla as "Kelly." He commands a mine-laying submarine, which pays frequent visits to the district patrolled by the American destroyers. When he has finished his task of distributing his mines where they will do the most harm, he generally devotes a few minutes to a prank of some sort. Sometimes, it is a note flying from a buoy, scribbled in schoolboy English, and addressed to his American enemy. On other occasions Kelly and his men leave the submarine and saunter along a desolate stretch of Irish shoreline, always leaving behind them a placard or other memento of their visit.

But the most hazardous exploit, according to gossip of American forecastles, was a visit which Kelly made to Dublin, remaining, it is said, for two days at one of the principal hotels, and later rejoining his boat somewhere on the west coast.

His latest feat was to visit an Irish village and plant the German flag on a rise of land above the town. One may imagine how the Irish fisherfolk, who have suffered from mines, treated this flag and how ardently they wished that flag were the body of Kelly.

But Kelly and his less humorously inclined commanders have been having a diminishing stock of enjoyment at the expense of the Allied navies in the past year. Senator Swanson, acting chairman of the Naval Committee in Congress, said on June 6, after a conference with Secretary Daniels and his assistants, that the naval forces of the Entente Powers had destroyed 60 per cent of all German submarines constructed, and that they had cut the shipping losses in half. Lloyd George in his great speech last July, said that 150 submarines had been sunk since war began and of this number 75 were sunk in the past 12 months. Truly an extraordinary showing.

CHAPTER VIII

PERILS AND TRIUMPHS OF SUBMARINE-HUNTING—THE LOSS OF OUR FIRST WAR-SHIP, THE CONVERTED GUNBOAT "ALCEDO"—BRAVERY OF CREW—"CASSIN" STRUCK BY TORPEDO, BUT REMAINS IN THE FIGHT—LOSS OF THE "JACOB JONES"—SINKING OF THE "SAN DIEGO"—DESTROYERS "NICHOLSON" AND "FANNING" CAPTURE A SUBMARINE, WHICH SINKS—CREW OF GERMANS BROUGHT INTO PORT—THE POLICY OF SILENCE IN REGARD TO SUBMARINE-SINKINGS

BUT as in the pursuit of dangerous game there is always liable to be two angles to any experience—or say, rather, a reverse angle, such as the hunted turning hunter—so in the matter of our fight against the submarine there are instances—not many, happily—where the U-boat has been able to deal its deadly blow first.

The first of our war-ships to be sunk by a submarine was the naval patrol gun-boat *Alcedo*, which was torpedoed shortly before 2 o'clock on the morning of November 5, 1917, almost exactly seven months after we entered the war. She was formerly G. W. Childs Drexel's yacht *Alcedo*, and Anthony J. Drexel

Paul, an officer in the Naval Reserve, was on her at the time. The vessel was the flag-ship of one of the patrol-flotillas, and for months had performed splendid service in the North Sea.

The torpedo that sunk the vessel came without warning, and so true was the aim that the war-ship went down in four minutes, carrying with her one officer and twenty of the crew. Commander William T. Conn, U. S. N., who commanded the vessel, in telling later of the experience, paid a high testimonial to the coolness and bravery of the crew. Eighty per cent of the men were reserves, but regulars could have left no better record of courage and precision.

"Here," said Commander Conn, "is a story that indicates the kind of men we have in the navy. I had a young lad in my crew, a yeoman, and one day I sent for him and told him that if we were ever torpedoed he was to save the muster-roll, so that when it was all over it would be possible to check up and find who had been saved. Well, the *Alcedo* was torpedoed at 2 o'clock one morning, and in four minutes she disappeared forever. Hours afterward, when we were waiting to be picked up, I saw my yeoman, and I said:

"'Son, where is my muster-roll?'

"'Here it is,' he replied, as he reached inside his shirt and pulled it out. ... And that same boy, in the terrible minutes that followed the loss of our ship, found a broken buoy. He was holding on to it when he saw one of our hospital stewards, who was about to give in. He struggled to the side of the steward and with one hand held him above the water while with the other he clung to the buoy. He held on until both were saved."

While the *Alcedo* was the first war-vessel to be sunk by a submarine, the first war-ship to be stricken in torpedo attack was the destroyer *Cassin*, one of the vessels that raced out of Newport to rescue the victims of the ravages of the German U-boat off Nantucket, in October, 1916. The *Cassin* was on patrol duty and had sighted a submarine about four miles away. The destroyer, in accordance with custom, headed for the spot, and had about reached it when the skipper, Commander Walter H. Vernou, sighted a torpedo running at high speed near the surface, and about 400 yards away. The missile was headed straight for the midship section of the war-ship. Realizing the situation, the commanding officer rang for the emergency full speed ahead on both engines, put the rudder hard over, and was just clear of the torpedo's course when it broached on the water, turned sharply and headed for the stern of the vessel. Here stood Osmond Kelly Ingram, gunner's mate, at his gun. He saw that if the torpedo struck at the stern it would, aside from working initial damage, cause the explosion of munitions stored on the after deck.

Thereupon, knowing that the torpedo was going to strike about where he stood, he ran to the pile of munitions and tumbled them into the sea. The explosion occurred as he was at work, and he was blown into the ocean and lost. But he had not died in vain, for the secondary explosion that he feared was averted by his act of supreme sacrifice.

Fortunately, only one engine was disabled by the explosion, and the destroyer was thus permitted to remain under way. She zigzagged to and fro, hoping to get a chance at her assailant, and in about an hour the German submarine commander decided that it was a good time to come to the surface for a better look at the destroyer. As the conning-tower came into view the *Cassin's* gunners delivered four shots, two of which fell so close to the U-boat that she submerged and was not seen again. In the meantime the crew, with splendid team-work, set about repairing the damage and attending to the five men who were wounded, none seriously.

After a while British war-ships came up and the *Cassin* returned to port. Admiral Sims mentioned Commander Vernou and his officers in despatches to Secretary Daniels, and more than a score of the seamen were cited for coolness and efficiency.

Our second war-ship definitely known to be sunk by the German submarines was the destroyer *Jacob Jones*, which was struck at 4.12 o'clock on the afternoon of December 6, last. The destroyer was on patrol, and nothing was known of the proximity of the submarine until the torpedo hit the vessel. The *Jacob Jones*, which was commanded by Lieutenant-Commander David Worth Bagley, a brother-in-law of Secretary Daniels and brother of Ensign Worth Bagley, who was killed on the torpedo-boat *Winslow* in the fight at Cardenas in the Spanish-American War, went down in seventeen minutes after she was struck. Gunner Harry R. Hood was killed by the explosion, but the remainder of the company got safely overside in rafts and boats. The submarine appeared after the sinking and took one of the survivors aboard as a prisoner. Lieutenant-Commander Bagley, with five others, landed in a small boat on the Scilly Islands while other survivors reached shore in various ways. The *Jacob Jones* was regarded by superstitious navy men as something of a Jonah, she having figured in one or two incidents involving German spies while in this country.

The first and to date the only American warship lost in American waters as a result of submarine attack was the armored cruiser *San Diego*—formerly the *California*—which was sunk by a mine off Point o' Woods on the Long Island coast on the morning of July 19,

1918. Facts associated with the disaster, involving the loss of some fifty lives, are illuminated with the light of supreme heroism, gallantry, and utter devotion. In no single instance was there failure on the part of officers or crew to meet the unexpected test in a manner quite in accordance with the most glorious annals of the United States Navy.

Point will perhaps be given to this if we picture Captain Harley H. Christie pushing his way about the welter of wreckage in a barrel, reorganizing some 800 of his men, who were floating about on every conceivable sort of object, into the disciplined unit that they had comprised before they were ordered overside to take their chances in the ocean. Or again, taking the enlisted-man aspect of the situation, there was the full-throated query of a husky seaman, clinging to a hatch as the *San Diego* disappeared:

"Where's the captain?"

Then a chorus of voices from the water:

"There he is! See his old bald head! God bless it! Three cheers for the skip!"

There they all were, some 800 men, survivors

of a company numbering thirteen-odd hundred, in the water, out of sight of land, not a ship in sight—and twelve life-boats among them, cheering, singing, exchanging badinage and words of good hope.

The *San Diego*, which was one of the crack shooting-ships of the navy, and had made seven round trips to France in convoy work without ever having seen a submarine, was on her way from the Portsmouth, N. H., navy-yard, where she had been completely overhauled in dry-dock and coaled, to New York, where her crew were to have had short liberty, preliminary to another voyage to France. She carried a heavy deck-load of lumber which she was to take to France for the Marine Corps. She had in her bunkers some 3,000 tons of coal.

On the morning of July 19, the cruiser, shortly after 11 o'clock, had reached a point about seven miles southeast of Point o' Woods. The sun was shining brilliantly, but the coast-line was veiled in a heavy haze. There was a fair ground-swell running, but no sea. The *San Diego* was ploughing along at a fifteen-knot clip, not pursuing the zigzag course which it is customary for vessels to follow in enemy-infested waters.

No submarine warning had been issued, and, as the vessel was only seven miles offshore, there may be no doubt that the officers of the war-ship did not consider the trip as any more hazardous than the hundreds of journeys she had made along our coast from port to port. The crew were engaged in the usual routine, with the added labor of getting the vessel ship-shape after the grimy operation of coaling at Portsmouth. The explosion came without warning at 11.15 o'clock. It was extremely heavy, accompanied by a rending and grinding of metal and by the explosion of the after-powder magazine, which destroyed the quarter-deck and sent the mainmast, with wireless attached, crashing overboard. The torpedo, or whatever it was, wrecked the engine-room, demolished the boilers, and put the electric dynamos out of order.

The thunderous explosion was followed immediately by the insistent whine of bugles and the clanging of alarm-bells, calling the crew to battle-stations. And the crew went quietly,

"ABANDON SHIP!" 165

without the slightest disorder. Down in the bunkers, four decks below, was an officer, with a party of seamen, setting things to rights after the coaling. As the explosion occurred and the vessel heeled, these men, as though instinctively, formed into a line, and then without excitement or hurry climbed the four upright steel ladders to the deck, the officer, of course, following last of all.

On deck the 6-inch starboard and port batteries were blazing away, not only at objects that might turn out to be periscopes or submarines, but in order to call assistance; for the wireless was out of commission, and there was not a sail or a hull in sight.

After a few minutes, the bugles sounded the order "Prepare to abandon ship." This applied to every one but the gun crews, who had to remain at their stations for at least five minutes after the process of abandonment was put into operation. The post of one of the guncrew officers was in the fighting-top of the basket-mast forward, his duty being that of spotter of his crew. As he hurried along the deck to his station the crew lined up along the port rail with life-preservers and were jumping into the sea as ordered.

There were comrades who had been killed or maimed by the shifting deck-load of lumber; there were comrades who, in jumping into the sea, had struck their heads against the steel hull, breaking their necks, and yet there the rest stood in line, waiting for the orders that would send them overboard.

"Isn't this a crime," laughed one of the seamen, "just after I had got on my liberty blues and was all set for the high spots in New York!"

"Cripes! My cigarettes are all wet! Who's got a dry one?"

"Look out there, kid; be careful you don't get your feet wet."

Twelve life-boats were overside, set adrift in the usual manner to be filled after the men were in the water. Then, of course, the sea was littered with lumber and all sorts of débris which would keep a man afloat.

While the abandonment of the ship was under way, the officer who had been in the bunkers, and whose station was in the fighting-top, hurried upward to his post. The port guns were still being served, but their muzzles were inclining ever downward toward the water. In his battle-station this officer directed the firing of the port guns until their muzzles dipped beneath the surface of the sea. There were three officers with him in the fighting-top and three seamen. Below they saw the perfect order which obtained, the men stepping into the sea in ranks, laughing and cheering.

Presently this officer sent one of the seamen down the mast to get life-belts for the group of men in the spotting-station. By the time he returned the bugles were ordering the total abandonment of the vessel.

So the little group made their way, not to the deck, which was now straight up and down, but to the starboard side of the hull, upon which they could walk, the vessel then being practically on her beam ends. Trapped at their stations on the port side were members of the 6-inch port battery. One of them was seen by a comrade just before rising waters shut him from view. The sinking man nodded and waved his hand.

"Good-by, Al," he said.

As the officer who had been in the fighting-top jumped clear into the sea, the vessel began to go down, now by the head. Slowly the stern rose, and as it did so, he says, the propellers came into view, and perched on one of the blades was a devil-may-care American seaman, waving his hat and shouting.

The vessel, the officer says, disappeared at 11.30 o'clock, fifteen minutes after the explosion occurred. There was some suction as the *San Diego* disappeared, but not enough, according to the calculation of the survivors with whom I talked, to draw men to their death.

In the course of another hour, Captain Christie had collected as many of his officers as he could, and the work of apportioning the survivors to the twelve boats and to pieces of flotsam was carried on with naval precision. One man, clinging to a grating, called out that he had cramps. A comrade in one of the boats thereupon said the sailor could have his place. He leaped into the sea and the man with cramps was assisted into the boat.

While this was going on a seaplane from the

CAPTAIN CHRISTIE 169

Bay Shore station passed over the heads of the men in the water. The seamen did not think they had been seen, but they had been, and the aviator, flying to Point o' Woods, landed and used the coast-guard telephone to apprise the Fire Island coast-guards of the disaster. From this station word was sent broadcast by wireless. In the meantime, Captain Christie had picked two crews of the strongest seamen and had them placed in No. 1 and No. 2 lifeboats. These men were ordered to row southwest to Fire Island and summon assistance.

In one boat thirteen men were placed; in the other fourteen. As the captain got the boat-crews arranged, his barrel began to get waterlogged and became rather precarious as a support; whereupon a floating seaman pushed his way through the water with a ladder.

"Here, sir," he said, "try this."

Thus it was that Captain Christie transferred to a new flag-ship.

The boat-crews left the scene of the disaster at 12.35, and they rowed in fifteen-minute relays from that hour until quarter past three. Before they had gone four miles merchant ships were rushing to the spot, as set forth in the wireless warning. These merchantmen got all of the men afloat in the water—or a vast majority of them—and took them to the naval station at Hoboken.

At the time of the disaster and for twenty-four hours thereafter there was some doubt whether or not the *San Diego* had been lost through contact with a mine, or was struck by a torpedo launched from a submarine. Submarine activities off Cape Cod the following Sunday, however, gave proof that the undersea boats had made their second hostile visit to our shores.

But later belief was that the cruiser was sunk by a mine planted by the submarine. One of our most illustrious exploits, indeed, occurred hardly a fortnight before the loss of the *Jones*, when two destroyers, the *Nicholson* and *Fanning*, steamed into their base with flags flying and German prisoners on their decks.

It was a clear November afternoon, and the destroyer *Fanning* was following her appointed route through the waters of the North Sea. Off to starboard the destroyer *Nicholson* was plunging on her way, throwing clouds of black smoke across the horizon. Near by was a merchant vessel, and the destroyers were engaged in taking her through the dangerous waters to safety. The air was so clear that minutest objects on the horizon were easily picked up by the questing binoculars of the men on watch. Suddenly came a cry from one of the forward lookouts:

"Periscope, two points off the starboard bow!"

The call sounded from stem to stern, and instantly the alarm to general quarters was sounded while the helm was thrown hard over. The signalman bent over his flag-locker and, in compliance with the order of the commander, bent flags onto the halyards, giving the location of the submarine to the *Nicholson*, while heliograph flashes from the bridge summoned her to joint attack. The waters were smooth, with a long swell, and the lookout had seen a scant eighteen inches of periscope, which had vanished immediately it fell under his vision. Undoubtedly the observer at the other end of the submarine's periscope had seen the *Fanning* at about the same time the presence of the undersea craft was detected. It had appeared about 400 yards from the destroyer's course.

In less time than it takes to tell, the *Fanning*, with throttles suddenly opened, plunged into the waters where the periscope had last been seen. And at the proper moment the commander, standing tensely on the bridge, released a depth-bomb from its fixed place. The explosive, 300 pounds in weight, sank with a gentle splash into the rolling wake of the destroyer and, at the depth as regulated before the bomb was released, it exploded with a terrific report.

Up from the ocean rose a towering column of water. It hung in the air for a moment like a geyser, and then gradually fell back to the level of the sea. A score of voices proclaimed the appearance of oil floating upon the water. Oil is sometimes released by a submarine to throw an attacking destroyer off the scent; but this time there were bubbles, too. That was quite significant. Then while the *Fanning* circled the spot wherein the explosion had occurred, the *Nicholson* stormed up, cut across the supposed lurking-place of the submarine, and released one of her depth charges. She, too, circled about the mass of boiling, oil-laden water.

For several minutes the two destroyers wheeled in and out like hawks awaiting their prey, and then suddenly there was a cry as a disturbance was noted almost directly between the two craft. The rush of water grew in volume until, as the men of the destroyers watched with all the ardor of fishermen landing trout, the U-boat came to the surface like a dead whale.

But the Americans were cautious. While stricken the undersea craft might show fight. So with guns and torpedo-tubes trained upon the submarine, they waited. But there was no fight in that boat. The depth charges had done their work thoroughly. While the visible portion of the hull appeared to have been uninjured, it was perfectly clear that the vessel was not under perfect control. Her ballast-tanks were damaged, which accounted for a bad list.

The explosions of the depth-bombs had hurled her to the bottom, where she retained sufficient buoyancy to catapult to the surface. As the conning-tower came into sight the *Nicholson* fired three shots from her stern gun. The U-boat then seemed to right herself, making fair speed ahead. The *Fanning* headed in toward her, firing from the bow gun. After the third shot the crew of the German vessel came up on deck, their hands upraised.

While approaching the craft both the destroyers kept their guns trained for instant use, but, as it turned out, precautions were unnecessary. Lines were thrown aboard the submersible and were made fast; but the U-boat, either stricken mortally or scuttled by her crew, began to settle. Lines were hastily cast off, and the boat sought her long rest upon the bottom of a sea to which no doubt she had sent many harmless vessels.

The crew of the U-boat, all of whom had life-preservers about their waists, leaped into the water and swam to the *Fanning ;* most of them were exhausted when they reached the destroyer's side. As the submarine sank, five or six men were caught in the wireless gear and carried below the surface before they disen-

RESCUE OF GERMANS

tangled themselves. Ten of the men were so weak that it was necessary to pass lines under their arms to haul them aboard. One man was in such a state that he could not even hold the line that was thrown to him.

Chief Pharmacist's Mate Elzer Howell and Coxswain Francis G. Connor thereupon jumped overboard and made a line fast to the German. But he died a few minutes after he was hauled aboard.

Once aboard, the prisoners were regaled with hot coffee and sandwiches, and so little did they mind the change to a new environment that, according to official Navy Department report, they began to sing. They were fitted with warm clothes supplied by the American sailors, and in other ways made to feel that, pirates though they were, and murderers as well, the American seafaring man knew how to be magnanimous.

The submarine bore no number nor other distinguishing marks, but her life-belts were marked on one side "Kaiser," and on the other "Gott." The *Fanning* steamed to port at high speed, and at the base transferred the prisoners under guard, who as they left the destroyer gave three lusty hochs for the *Fanning's* men. Then the *Fanning* put out to sea a few miles, and after the young American commander had read the burial service, the body of the German seaman who had died was committed to the depths. The commander of the *Fanning* was Lieutenant A. S. Carpender, a Jerseyman, who in his report gave particular praise to Lieutenant Walter Henry, officer of the deck, and to Coxswain Loomis, who first sighted the submarine.

This was by no means the first time a submarine had been sunk by an American destroyer, but in accordance with the British policy, the Americans had withheld all information of the sort. However, this was such a good story, and the capture of prisoners so unusual, that by agreement between the Navy Department and the British Admiralty, the salient details of this encounter were given to the public.

The idea of secrecy was devised by the British at the very outset, the purpose being to make the waging of submarine warfare doubly objectionable to the men of the German Navy. It is bad enough to be lost in a naval engagement, but at least the names of the ships involved and the valor of the crews, both friend and enemy, are noted. But under the British system, a submarine leaves port, and if she is sunk by a patrol-vessel or other war-ship, that fact is never made known. The Germans know simply that still another submarine has entered the great void.

It adds a sinister element to an occupation sufficiently sinister in all its details. There may be no doubt that the policy of silence has had its effect upon the German morale. That crews have mutinied on the high seas is undoubted, while we know of several mutinies involving hundreds of men that have occurred in German ports—all because of objections to submarine service. It is even said that submarine service is now one of the penalties for sailors who have offended against the German naval regulations, and there are stories of submarines decked with flowers as they leave port, a symbol, of course, of men who go out not expecting to return—all for the glory of the man known throughout the American Navy as "Kaiser Bill."

It is thus unlikely that such success as might

—or may—attend the efforts of our coast-patrol vessels to dispose of the submarines which come here will not be published unless the highly colored complexion of facts warrants it. One may imagine that service in a submarine so far from home is not alluring, and still less so when submarines sent to the waters of this hemisphere are heard from nevermore.

Just how unpopular the service has been may be adduced from chance remarks of German submarine prisoners who come to this country from time to time. The men of the U-boat sunk by the *Fanning* made no effort to conceal their satisfaction at their change of quarters, while Germans in other cases have told their British captors that they were glad they had been taken.

There is the story of the storekeeper of the German submarine which sunk several vessels off our coast last June. He said he had formerly served on a German liner plying between Hoboken and Hamburg, and his great regret was that he had not remained in this country when he had a chance. Life on a submarine, he said, was a dog's life.

HARD LIFE ON SUBMARINE 179

Even under peace conditions this is so. The men are cramped for room, in the first place. In a storm the vessel, if on the surface, is thrown almost end over end, while the movement of stormy waves affects a boat even thirty feet below the water-level. Cooking is very often out of the question, and the men must live on canned viands. They have not even the excitement of witnessing such encounters as the vessel may have. Three men only, the operating officers, look through the periscope; the others have their stations and their various duties to perform. If a vessel is sunk they know it through information conveyed by their officers. There was a story current in Washington before we entered the war, of a sailor, a German sailor who had had nearly a year of steady service on a submarine. He was a faithful man, and as he was about to go ashore on a long leave, his commanding officer asked what he could do for him.

"Only one thing," was the reply. "Let me have one look through the periscope."

In the past year the Allies have been employing their own submarines in the war against the

German undersea peril. This has been made possible by the perfection of the listening device before referred to by which the presence of a submarine and other details may be made known. But it is a dangerous business at best, and not largely employed, if only for the reason that patrol-vessels are not always likely to distinguish between friend and foe. We have in mind the tragic instance of the American cruiser which fired upon a submarine in the Mediterranean, killing two men, only to find that the vessel was an Italian undersea boat. Of course our deepest regrets were immediately forthcoming, and were accepted by the Italian Government in like spirit.

CHAPTER IX

OUR BATTLESHIP FLEET—GREAT WORKSHOP OF WAR—PREPARATIONS FOR FOREIGN SERVICE—ON A BATTLESHIP DURING A SUBMARINE ATTACK—THE WIRELESS THAT WENT WRONG—THE TORPEDO THAT MISSED—ATTACK ON SUBMARINE BASES OF DOUBTFUL EXPEDIENCY—WHEN THE GERMAN FLEET COMES OUT—ESTABLISHMENT OF STATION IN THE AZORES

WHEN the German fleet of battleships and battle-cruisers sallies forth into the North Sea for a final fight against the British Grand Fleet, they will find American dreadnoughts and superdreadnoughts ready and eager to lend the material weight of their assistance to the Allied cause. A substantial number of our capital ships, under command of Rear-Admiral Hugh Rodman, are with the Grand Fleet, and have been for some months. Both in Washington and in London a German sea offensive on a grand scale has long been regarded as a possibility, and the admiralty authorities at the Entente capitals are anxious for the supreme test, and confident concerning its outcome. We have already noted Admiral Beatty's action in assigning American battleships to the place of honor in the line of sea-fighters which went forth to meet a reported German attack some time ago. It was a false report, but the honor done our naval fighters stands.

The expansion of the United States Navy has also included an enormous increase in our battleships and battle-cruisers; definite details are withheld, but it is not too much to say that we are thoroughly equipped to assist Great Britain very vitally in this respect. In the summer of 1917 Secretary Daniels announced that the Atlantic Fleet—our Grand Fleet—had been reorganized into two divisions, officially known as "forces." Battleship Force One had as commander Vice-Admiral Albert W. Grant, and Battleship Force Two was commanded by Vice-Admiral DeWitt Coffman. Admiral Henry T. Mayo remained as commander-in-chief.

"There are," said Secretary Daniels in announcing the new arrangement—July 18, 1917—"twice as many battleships in commission as we ever had before; in fact, every battleship we have is in commission. The whole purpose of the new organization is to keep our battleship fleet in as perfect condition as possible, to put it in the highest state of efficiency and readiness for action."

Eventually an appreciable number of our best fighters were sent to the Grand Fleet—which, however, is by no means to be understood as implying that our own coasts are unprotected. Not at all. The Navy Department has a viewpoint which embraces all possible angles, and nothing in the way of precaution has been overlooked. At the same time it has been the theory of Secretary Daniels that the way to beat the submarine and the German Navy in general was to go to the base of things, "to the neck of the bottle," and this as much as anything—more, in sooth—accounts for the hundreds of war-ships of various sorts that now fly our flag in the war zone.

The orders dividing the fleet into two "forces" and despatching a representation of our greatest fighters to the North Sea was preceded by a period of preparation the like of which this country—perhaps the world—never saw. The Atlantic Fleet was, indeed, converted into a huge workshop of war, turning out its finished products—fighting men. A visitor to the fleet, writing under date of May 14, expressed amazement at the amount of well-ordered activity which characterized a day on every one of the battleships. Here were men being trained for armed-guard service on merchantmen, groups of neophytes on the after deck undergoing instruction on the loading-machines; farther along a group of qualified gunners were shattering a target with their 5-inch gun. Other groups were hidden in the turrets with their long 14 and 12 inch guns, three or two to a turret. Signal-flags were whipping the air aloft—classes in signalling; while from engine-room and fighting-tops each battleship hummed with the activities of masters and pupils teaching and learning every phase of the complicated calling of the modern navy man.

And there were days when the great fleet put to sea for target practice and for battle manœuvres, the turrets and broadsides belching forth their tons upon tons of steel and the observers aloft sending down their messages of commendation for shots well aimed. It is the statement of those in a position to know that never were jackies so quick to learn as those of our war-time personnel. Whether the fact of war is an incentive, or whether American boys are adapted, through a life of competitive sport, quickly to grasp the sailorman's trade, the truth remains that in a very short space the boy who has never seen a ship develops swiftly into a bluejacket, rolling, swaggering, but none the less deft, precise, and indomitable.

"They come into the navy to fight," said one of the officers of the fleet, "and they want to get into the thick of it. We turn out qualified gun crews in three months—and that is going some. A large majority of the new men of the fleet come from farms, especially from the Middle West. More than 90 per cent of the seamen are native-born, and on any ship may be heard the Southern drawl, the picturesque vernacular of the lower East or West side of New York City, the twang of New England, the rising intonation of the Western Pennsylvanian, and that indescribable vocal cadence that comes only from west of Chicago.

Not only gunners were developed, but engineers, electricians, cooks, bakers—what-not?

They are still being developed on our home ships, but in the meantime the fruits of what was done in the time dating from our entrance into the war to the present summer are to be noted chiefly in the North Sea, where our vessels lie waiting with their sisters of the British Fleet for the appearance of the German armada.

Let us transfer ourselves for the time being from the general to the particular: in other words, to the deck of a great American dreadnought, which, together with others of her type, has been detached from the Atlantic Fleet and assigned to duty with Admiral Beatty's great company of battleships and battle-cruisers. This battleship has entered the war zone, en route to a certain rendezvous, whence all the American units will proceed to their ultimate destination in company.

It is night. It is a black night. The stars are viewless and the ocean through which the great steel hull is rushing, with only a slight hiss where the sharp cutwater parts the waves, is merely a part of the same gloom. Aloft and on deck the battleship is a part of the night. Below deck all is dark save perchance a thin, knife-like ray emanating from a battle-lantern. The lookouts, straining their eyes into the black for long, arduous stretches, are relieved and half-blind and dizzy they grope along the deck to their hammocks, stumbling over the prostrate forms of men sleeping beside the 5-inch guns, exchanging elbow thrusts with those of the gun crews who are on watch.

The trip this far has been a constant sucession of drills and instruction in the art of submarine fighting—all to the tune of general alarm and torpedo defense bells. And the while preparations for sighting the enemy have never been minimized. They involved precautions not dissimilar to those on board a destroyer or other patrol-vessel, but were of course conducted on a vastly greater scale. As suggesting an outline of measures of watchfulness, we may regard this battleship as the centre of a pie, with special watches detailed to cover their given slice of this pie. These slices are called water sectors, and each sector, or slice, extends at a given angle from the course of the ship out to the horizon. Of course as the vessel is constantly moving at a rapid rate, the centre of the pie shifts, too. In this way every foot of water within the great circle of the horizon is under constant supervision night and day by a small army of lookouts, armed with binoculars and gun telescopes.

And so our battleship goes on through the night. On the bridge all is quiet. Officers move to and fro with padded footfalls, and the throb of the great engines is felt rather than heard. The wind begins to change, and presently the captain glancing out the door of the chart-house clucks his chagrin. For the night has begun to reveal itself, thanks, or rather, no thanks, to the moon, which has torn away from a shrouding mass of clouds and sends its rays down upon the waters of the sea. It had been a fine night to dodge the lurking submarine, but now the silver light of the moon, falling upon the leaden side of the battleship, converts her into a fine target.

"Nature is certainly good to the Germans," chuckles an officer to a companion, taking care that the captain does not hear."

"Yes," comes the sententious reply. The lookouts grow more rigid, for whereas formerly they could see nothing, objects on the water are now pencilled out in luminous relief.

Deep down below the water there is a listening "ear"—a submarine telephone device through which a submarine betrays its presence; any sound the undersea boat makes, the beating of the propellers, for instance, is heard by this ear, and in turn by the ear of the man who holds the receiver.

Presently the man who is on detector watch grows tense. He listens attentively and then stands immobile for a moment or so. Then he steps to a telephone and a bell rings in the charthouse where the captain and his navigating and watch officers are working out the courses and positions.

"I hear a submarine signalling, sir," comes the voice from the depths to the captain who stands by the desk with the receiver at his ear.

"What signal?" barks the skipper.

"'M Q' repeated several times. Sounds as if one boat was calling another." (The sailor referred to the practice which submarines have of sending subaqueous signals to one another, signals which are frequently caught by listening war-ships of the Allies.)

The captain orders the detector man to miss nothing, and then a general alarm (to quarters) is passed through the great vessel by word of mouth. This is no time for the clanging of bells and the like. The lookouts are advised as to the situation.

"I hope we're not steaming into a nest." The captain frowns and picks up the telephone. "Anything more?" he asks.

"Still getting signals, sir; same as before; same direction and distance."

Down to the bridge through a speaking-tube, running from the top of the forward basket-mast comes a weird voice.

"Bright light, port bow, sir. Distance about 4,000 yards." (Pause.) "Light growing dim. Very dim now."

From other lookouts come confirmatory words.

"Dim light; port bow."

"The light has gone."

"It's a sub, of course," murmurs an officer. "No craft but a submarine would carry a night light on her periscope. She must be signalling."

A thrill goes through the battleship. In a minute the big steel fighter may be lying on her side, stricken; or there may be the opportunity for a fair fight.

The captain sends an officer below to the detector and changes the course of the ship. Every one awaits developments, tensely.

The wireless operator enters the chart-house.

"I can't get your message to the —— [another battleship], sir. I can't raise her. Been trying for ten minutes."

The officer who has been below at the detector comes up and hears the plight of the wireless man. He smiles.

"In exactly five minutes," he says, "you signal again." The radio man goes to his room and the officer descends to the detector. In precisely five minutes he hears the signal which had bothered the man on detector watch. He hurries to the bridge with the solution of the incident. The wireless had become disconnected and its signals had come in contact with the detector. So there was no submarine. Everything serene. The battleship settles down to her night routine.

The dark wears into dawn, and the early morning, with the dusk, is the favorite hunting-time of the submarine, for the reason that then a periscope, while seeing clearly, is not itself easily to be discerned. The lookouts, straining their eyes out over the steely surge, pick up what appears to be a spar. But no. The water is rushing on either side of it like a mill race. A periscope.

There is a hurry of feet on the bridge. The navigating officer seizes the engine-room telegraph and signals full speed ahead. While the ship groans and lists under the sudden turn at high speed, the ammunition-hoists drone as they bring powder and shell up to gun and turret. From the range-finding and plotting-stations come orders to the sight-setters, and in an instant there is a stupendous roar as every gun on the port side sends forth its steel messenger.

Again and again comes the broadside, while the ocean for acres about the periscope boils with the steel rain. It is much too hot for the submarine which sinks so that the periscope is invisible. From the plotting-stations come orders for a change of range, and on the sea a

"TORPEDO!"

mile or so away rise huge geysers which pause for a moment, glistening in the light of the new sun, and then fall in spray to the waves, whence they were lifted by the hurtling projectiles. The shells do not ricochet. "Where they hit they dig," to quote a navy man. This is one of the inventions of the war, the non-ricochet shell. One may easily imagine how greatly superior are the shells that dig to those that strike the water and then glance. Then comes the cry:

"Torpedo!"

All see it, a white streak upon the water, circling from the outer rim of shell-fire on a wide arc, so as to allow for the speed of the battleship. With a hiss the venomous projectile dashes past the bow, perhaps thirty yards away. Had not the battleship swung about on a new course as soon as the vigilant lookout descried the advancing torpedo, it would have been a fair hit amidships. As it was, the explosive went harmlessly on its way through the open sea. A short cheer from the crew marks the miss, and the firing increases in intensity. The battleship so turns that her bow is in the direction of the submarine, presenting, thus, a mark which may be hit only through a lucky shot, since the submarine is a mile away. Accurate shooting even at a mile is expected of torpedo-men when the mark is a broadside, but hitting a "bow-on" object is a different matter.

Two more torpedoes zip past, and then over the seas comes bounding a destroyer, smoke bellying from her funnels. She is over the probable hiding-place of the submarine, and a great explosion and a high column of water tell those on the battleship that she has released a depth-bomb. Suddenly a signal flutters to the stay of the destroyer. The crew of the battleship cheer. There is no more to fear from that submarine, for oil is slowly spreading itself over the surface of the ocean—oil and pieces of wreckage.

The dawn establishes itself fully. The battleship resumes her course toward the appointed rendezvous.

Our navy has always held the idea that the Germans could be routed out from their submarine bases, has believed that, after all, that is the one sure way of ridding the seas of the

Kaiser's pirates for good. It may be assumed that the recent attacks of the British upon Ostend and Zeebrugge, as a cover to blocking the canal entrances through sinking old war-ships, were highly approved by Vice-Admiral Sims. Secretary Daniels has considered the advisability of direct methods in dealing with the German Navy. No doubt the temptation has been great, if only because of the fact that with the British and American and French navies combined, we have a force which could stand an appreciable amount of destruction and yet be in a position to cope with the German fleet. Yet, of course, that is taking chances. And:

"It is all very well to say 'damn the torpedoes,'" said Secretary Daniels, in discussing this point, "but a navy cannot invite annihilation by going into mined harbors, and ships can do little or nothing against coast fortifications equipped with 14-inch guns. Experience at Gallipoli emphasizes this fact. And yet"— here the secretary became cryptic—"there is more than one way to kill a cat. No place is impregnable. Nothing is impossible."

The British showed how damage might be

dealt naval bases supposedly secure under the guns of fortifications, but something more than a sally will be necessary to smoke out the German fleet, or to root out the nests of submarines along the coast of Belgium. Again, there is the theory that eventually the Germans will come out and give battle. There is a psychological backing for this assumption, for the irksomeness of being penned up wears and wears until it is not to be borne. At least this seems to have been the case in blockades in past wars, notably the dash of Admiral Cervera's squadron from Santiago Harbor.

But when the Germans come it will be no such forlorn hope as that—at least not according to the German expectation; what they expect, however, and what they may get are contingencies lying wide apart.

In connection with our far-flung naval policy the establishment of a naval base on the Azores Islands was announced last spring. The arrangement was made with the full consent of Portugal, and the design was the protection of the Atlantic trade routes to southern Europe. Guns have already been landed on the island,

THE AZORES STATION

and fortifications are now in process of construction. The station, besides being used as a naval base for American submarines, destroyers, and other small craft, will serve as an important homing-station for our airplanes, a number of which have already been assembled there.

The establishment of this station greatly simplifies the task of protecting the great trade routes, not only to southern Europe and the Mediterranean, but also returning traffic to South American and southern Gulf ports in the United States.

CHAPTER X

THE GREAT ATLANTIC FERRY COMPANY, INCORPORATED, BUT UNLIMITED—FEAT OF THE NAVY IN REPAIRING THE STEAMSHIPS BELONGING TO GERMAN LINES WHICH WERE INTERNED AT BEGINNING OF WAR IN 1914—WELDING AND PATCHING—TRIUMPH OF OUR NAVY WITH THE "VATERLAND"—HER CONDITION—KNOTS ADDED TO HER SPEED—DAMAGE TO MOTIVE POWER AND HOW IT WAS REMEDIED—FAMOUS GERMAN LINERS BROUGHT UNDER OUR FLAG

IN an address delivered not long ago, Admiral Gleaves, commander-in-chief of the United States Cruiser and Transport Force, referred to "The Great Atlantic Ferry Company, Incorporated, but Unlimited." He referred to our transport fleet, of course, a fleet which, under naval supervision and naval operation, has safely transported more than a million of our soldiers to France. When the history of the war finally comes to be written, our success in the handling of oversea transportation will not be the least bright among the pages of that absorbing history.

When the European nations first went to war in 1914 I happened to be at the Newport Naval

Training Station, and I asked an officer what would happen if we went into the war.

"Not much," he said. "We would stand on our shores and the Germans on theirs and make faces at each other."

Events have proved that he was not looking into the future wisely, not taking into account the enormous energy and get-things-doneness of Secretary Daniels and his coadjutors. Not only did the Navy Department send our destroyer fleet to the war zone—the Allied officers, believing co-operation of the sort not feasible, had neither requested nor expected this—but performed many other extraordinary feats, among them the equipping of transports to carry our men to France, and the conduct of the service when they were ready.

We had only a fair number of American steamships adapted for the purpose, but lying in our ports were interned German and Austrian vessels aggregating many hundreds of thousands of tons. From 1914 until we entered the war commuters on North River ferry-boats seemed never weary of gazing at the steamships lying in the great North German Lloyd and Hamburg-

American line piers in Hoboken. There was a small forest of masts and funnels appearing above the pier sheds, while many a graceful stern protruded out beyond the pier lines into the river.

Among them was the great *Vaterland*, the largest vessel in the world, and the outward and visible expression of that peaceful maritime rivalry between Great Britain and the German Empire, which in the transatlantic lanes as in the waters of all the seven seas had interested followers of shipping for so many years. There was, so far as passenger traffic was concerned, the rivalry for the blue ribbon of the sea—the swiftest ocean carrier, a fight that was waged between Great Britain and Germany from the placid eighties to the nineties, when the Germans brought out the *Deutschland*, and later the *Kaiser Wilhelm der Grosse*, the *Kaiser Wilhelm II*—all champions—whose laurels were to be snatched away by the *Mauretania* and the *Lusitania*—the two speed queens—when war ended competition of the sort.

But the contest in speed had, to an extent, been superseded by the rivalry of size, a struggle begun by the White Star Line when the great *Oceanic* slipped past quarantine in the early 1900's, and carried on by that line, by the Atlantic Transport Line, and by the German companies with unceasing vigor. Great carrying capacity and fair speed were the desiderata, and the studious Germans were quick to see that it was a far more profitable battle to wage, since speed meant merely advertising, with a more or less slight preponderance in the flow of passenger patronage to the line which owned the latest crack greyhound, whereas size meant ability to carry greater cargoes, and thus enhanced earning capacity.

So great hulls were the order of the years preceding 1914. There came the new *Baltic*, the new *Cymric*, the new *Adriatic* of the White Star Line, and for the Germans there came the *Amerika* and other craft of that type. Finally there was the *Titanic* and her ill-fated maiden voyage; the Cunarder *Aquitania*, and the *Vaterland*, and the *Imperator*, which bore the German ensign. These facts, presented not altogether in chronological order, are necessary to give the reader an idea of the manner in which the Americans were taking back seats in the unceasing fight for commercial maritime supremacy. It is quite likely, so far back was our seat, that the Germans held little respect for our ability, either to man or to fit the immense number of German vessels in our harbors. In truth, the events that followed our entrance into the war showed just how supreme the contempt of the Germans was for our knowledge of things nautical.

We are about to record just how erroneous that attitude of the Germans was, but wish first to point out that they had failed to take into consideration the fact that at Annapolis is situated a school of the sea that asks nothing of any similar school in the world, and that they had also failed to note that, while we had not gone in heavily for shipping, we have been rather effective in other lines which in event of emergency might be brought to bear upon the problem of correcting such deficiencies as might exist in our store of modern nautical tradition.

Well, while the German waged their unrestricted warfare on the sea, those German vessels lay at Hoboken and at other ports of the country, gathering the rust and barnacles of disuse. Then one day Congress spoke definitely, and the next morning North River ferry voyagers saw lying off the German docks a torpedo-boat destroyer flying the American flag. Some days later the American flag floated over the taffrails of the *Vaterland*, the *Kaiser Wilhelm II*, and other Teutonic craft. Their employment in the way of providing transportation of our soldiers, of course, was contemplated. In fact, the accession to our marine of such a large number of hulls seemed to provide for us all the necessary means which otherwise we would have lacked.

But not so fast. When our officers began to look over these German craft they found that they were in a woful condition, not so much because of disuse as because of direct damage done to them by the German crews who had been attached to the ships ever since they were laid up in 1914. There is evidence in Washington that the German central authorities issued an order for the destruction of these ships which was to be effective on or about February 1, 1917—simultaneous, in other words, with the date set for unrestricted warfare. There is not the slightest doubt that the purpose of the order was to cause to be inflicted damage so serious to vital parts of the machinery of all German vessels in our ports, that no ship could be operated within a period of time ranging from eight months to two years, if at all.

But the Germans miscalculated, as already set forth. We took over the 109 German vessels in April, and by December 30 of that year, 1917, all damage done to them had been repaired and were in service, adding more than 500,000 tons gross to our transport and cargo fleets. In general the destructive work of the German crews consisted of ruin which they hoped and believed would necessitate the shipping of new machinery to substitute for that which was battered down or damaged by drilling or by dismantlement.

To have obtained new machinery, as a matter of fact, would have entailed a mighty long process. First, new machinery would have had to be designed, then made, and finally installed. These would have been all right if time was unlimited. But it was not; it was, on the other hand, extremely limited. The army wished to send troops abroad, the Allies were pleading for men, and the only way to get them over in time to do anything was to do quick repair jobs on the damaged vessels. But how? Investigation revealed how thorough the work of the German seamen—now enjoying themselves in internment camps—had been. Their destructive campaign had been under headway for two months, and they had thus plenty of time in which to do all sorts of harm, ranging from the plugging of steam-pipes to the demolition of boilers by dry firing.

The Shipping Board experts were the first to go over the German craft, and as a result of their survey it was announced that a great deal of new machinery would have to be provided, and that a fair estimate of the work of remedying the damage inflicted would be eighteen months. But this was too long, altogether so. The officers of the Navy Bureau of Steam Engineering took a hand, and finally decided that it would be possible to clear the ships for service by Christmas of that year. (As a matter of record, the last of the 109 ships was ordered into service on Thanksgiving Day.)

To accomplish the purposes they had in mind, the Navy Department engaged the services of all available machinery welders and patchers, many of whom were voluntarily offered by the great railroad companies. Most of the time that was required was due not so much to actual repair work as to the devious and tedious task of dismantling all machinery from bow to stern of every ship in order to make certain that every bit of damage was discovered and repaired. In this way all chance of overlooking some act of concealed mutilation was obviated.

It would appear that explosives were not used in the process of demolition by the Germans, but at the time the engineers could not be sure of this, and as a consequence as they worked they were conscious of the danger of hidden charges which might become operative when the machinery was put to the test, or even while the work of dismantling and inspection was being carried on. There were, however, discovered, as a result of this rigid investigation of every mechanical detail, many artful cases

From a photograph copyright by International Film Service.

Repairing a damaged cylinder of a German ship for federal service.

of pipe-plugging, of steel nuts and bolts concealed in delicate mechanical parts, of ground glass in oil-pipes and bearings, of indicators that were so adjusted as to give inaccurate readings, of fire-extinguishers filled with gasolene—in fact, the manifold deceits which the Germans practised would make a chapter of themselves.

Suffice to say, that through painstaking investigation every trick was discovered and corrected. On each vessel there was no boiler that was not threaded through every pipe for evidence of plugging, no mechanism of any sort that was not completely dismantled, inspected, and reassembled. On one ship the engineers chanced to find a written record of the damage inflicted. In every other case the search for evidence of sabotage was blind. This memorandum in the case of the one ship was evidently left on board through an oversight, and written in German, was a veritable guide-book for our engineers. In order that the reader may have some idea of the sort of damage done, the following extracts from that memorandum of destructiveness is herewith presented:

"Starboard and port high pressure cylinders with valve chest; upper exhaust outlet flange broken off. (Cannot be repaired.)"

"Starboard and port second intermediate valve chest; steam inlet flange broken off. (Cannot be repaired.)"

"First intermediate pressure starboard exhaust pipes of exhaust line to second intermediate pressure flange broken off. (Cannot be repaired.)"

"Starboard and port low pressure exhaust pipe damaged. (Cannot be repaired.)"

Naval officers are pleased to recall that every single one of these supposedly irreparable injuries was not only repaired, but speedily repaired. Patching and welding were the answer to the problem they presented. Both these valuable methods had never been employed in marine engineering, although they had been used by the railroads for some fifteen years. There are three methods; or, rather, three methods were employed: electric welding, oxyacetylene welding, and ordinary mechanical patching. After repairs were effected tests of the machinery were first made at the docks with the ships lashed to the piers, the propellers being driven at low speed. Later each vessel was taken to sea for vigorous trial tests, and everything was found to be perfectly satisfactory. Indeed, it has been asserted that several knots were added to the best speed that the *Vaterland*—renamed *Leviathan*—ever made.

Of course the crew of the *Vaterland* had spared no pains in fixing that great ship so that she could not be used; even so they had less to do than the engine forces of other craft, for the reason that the vessel was in extremely bad repair as she was. As a consequence, she was one of the German ships that were least mutilated. When repairs were completed and it was time for her trial trip, her commander, a young American naval officer, was ordered to test the big craft in every way, to utilize every pound of steam pressure, and to try her out to the limit. For, if there was anything wrong with the vessel, the navy wished to know it before she fared forth with troops on board.

The *Leviathan* stood the test. And to-day we all know what a great part she has played in carrying our soldiers to France. She is, in fact, a far better boat than on her maiden trip, for our engineers were surprised to find how sloppily she had been built in certain respects.

In preparing her for sea the engineers found it necessary to overhaul, partially redesign and reconstruct many important parts of the *Leviathan's* engines. As in her case, the most serious typical damage was done by breaking the cylinders, valve-chests, circulating pumps, steam and exhaust units in main engines; dry-firing boilers, and thus melting the tubes and distorting furnaces, together with easily detectable instances of a minor character, such as cutting piston and connecting rods and stays with hack saws, smashing engine-room telegraph systems, and removing and destroying parts which the Germans believed could not be duplicated. Then there was sabotage well concealed: rod stays in boilers were broken off, but nuts were fastened on exposed surfaces for purposes of deception; threads of bolts were destroyed, the bolts being replaced with but one or two threads to hold them, and thus calculated to give way under pressure. Piles of shavings and inflammable material with cans of kerosene near suggested the intention to burn the vessels, intentions thwarted by our watchfulness, while the absence of explosives has been accounted for purely on the ground of the risk which the crews would have run in attempting to purchase explosive materials in the open market.

No great amount of damage was done to the furnishings or ordinary ship's fittings. Destructiveness was similar in character throughout all the vessels and involved only important parts of the propulsive mechanism or other operating machinery.

We have spoken of the investigation of the vessels by Shipping Board engineers. They were appointed by the board not only to make a survey, but to superintend repairs. The collector of the port of New York also named a board of engineers (railroad engineers) to investigate the damage done the German ships, and to recommend repairs through the agency of welding. The railroad men, after due study, believed that their art could be applied to as great advantage on ships as upon locomotives. The Shipping Board engineers recommended, on the other hand, the renewal of all badly damaged cylinders. The railroad engineers, on the other hand, set forth their opinion that all damaged cylinders could be reclaimed and made as good as new.

As a result of this difference of opinion, nothing was done until the larger German craft were turned over to the Navy Department to be fitted as transports, in July of 1917. It was then decided to use welding and patching on the vessels.

In no cases were the repairs to the propulsive machinery delayed beyond the time necessary to equip these ships as transports. Electric and acetylene welding is not a complicated art in the hands of skilled men; for patching a hole, or filling the cavity of a great crack in a cylinder, say by electric welding, may be compared to a similar operation in dental surgery.

Returning to the *Leviathan's* faulty German construction, be it said that the opinion of the navy engineers who overhauled her, was that inferior engineering had been practised in her construction. There are on this craft four turbine engines ahead, and four astern, on four shafts. All the head engines were in good

THE *VATERLAND* 213

shape, but all the astern engines were damaged. But the main part of the damage had resulted more to faulty operation of the engines than to malicious damage. Cracks were found in the casing of the starboard high-pressure backing turbine, cracks of size so great as to make it certain that this engine had not been used in the last run of that vessel on transatlantic service in 1914. There was discovered on the *Vaterland*, or *Leviathan*, documentary evidence to prove this, and it also appeared from this paper that on her last trip to this country the vessel had not averaged twenty knots. It may be that the German ship-builders had hurried too swiftly in their strenuous efforts to produce a bigger, if not a better, steamship than the British could turn out.

Forty-six of the *Vaterland's* boilers showed evidence of poor handling. They were not fitted with the proper sort of internal feed-pipes. All these defects, defects original with the steamship, were repaired by the Americans. In addition, evidences of minor attempts to disable the *Vaterland* were found, such, for instance, as holes bored in sections of suction-pipes, the holes having been puttied and thus concealed. Things of the sort afforded ample reason for a thorough overhaul of the vast mass of machinery aboard the steamship. But eventually she was ready for her test and her performance on a trial trip to southern waters showed how skilful had been the remedial measures applied.

Aboard the *Leviathan* as other big German liners, such as the *Amerika*, *President Grant*, *President Lincoln* (recently sunk by a German torpedo while bound for this country from France), the *George Washington*, and other vessels fitted as troop and hospital ships, and the like, naval crews were placed, and naval officers, of course, in command. They have proved their mettle, all. They have shown, further, that when we get ready to take our place, after the war, among the nations that go in heavily for things maritime, we shall not be among the last, either in point of resourcefulness or intrepidity.

Civilian sailormen who have sailed on vessels commanded by naval officers have been inclined to smile over the minutia of navy discipline and have expressed doubt whether the naval

HANDLING THE *LEVIATHAN*

men would find a certain rigidity any more useful in a given situation than the civilian seamen would find a looser ordered system. We can but base judgment on facts, and among the facts that have come under the writer's observation, was the difficulty which the German officers of the *Vaterland* encountered in taking their vessel into her dock in the North River. The very last time they attempted it the great hulk got crosswise in the current in the middle of the stream, and caused all sorts of trouble.

Our naval officers, however, made no difficulty at all in snapping the steamship into her pier. She steams up the Hudson on the New York side, makes a big turn, and lo! she is safely alongside her pier. Any seafaring man will tell you that this implies seamanly ability.

Following is a list of the larger German ships which were repaired by the navy engineers, with the names under which they now sail:

FORMER NAME	PRESENT NAME
Amerika	*America.*
Andromeda	*Bath.*
Barbarossa	*Mercury.*
Breslau	*Bridgeport.*

FORMER NAME	PRESENT NAME
Cincinnati	Covington* (sunk).
Frieda Lenhardt	Astoria.
Friedrich der Grosse	Huron.
Geier	Schurz.
George Washington	name retained.
Grosser Kurfurst	Aeolus.
Grunewald	Gen. G. W. Goethals.
Hamburg	Powhattan.
Hermes	name retained.
Hohenfelde	Long Beach.
Kiel	Camden.
Kaiser Wilhelm II	Agamemnon.
Koenig Wilhelm II	Madawaska.
Kronprinz Wilhelm	Von Steuben.
Kronprezessin Cecelie	Mount Vernon.
Liebenfels	Hoiston.
Locksun	Gulfport.
Neckar	Antigone.
Nicaria	Pensacola.
Odenwald	Newport News.
Præsident	Kuttery.
President Grant	name retained.
President Lincoln	name retained (sunk).
Prinzess Irene	Pocahontas.
Prinz Eitel Friedrich	DeKalb.
Rhein	Susquehanna.
Rudolph Blumberg	Beaufort.
Saxonia	Savannah.
Staatsskretar	Samoa.
Vaterland	Leviathan.
Vogensen	Quincy.

*Is not this rather a reflection upon a perfectly good **American city**?

CHAPTER XI

CAMOUFLAGE—AMERICAN SYSTEM OF LOW VISIBILITY AND THE BRITISH DAZZLE SYSTEM—AMERICANS WORKED OUT PRINCIPLES OF COLOR IN LIGHT AND COLOR IN PIGMENT—BRITISH SOUGHT MERELY TO CONFUSE THE EYE—BRITISH SYSTEM APPLIED TO SOME OF OUR TRANSPORTS

WHILE our naval vessels, that is to say war-ships, have adhered to the lead-gray war paint, the Navy Department has not declined to follow the lead of the merchant marine of this country and Great Britain in applying the art of camouflage to some of its transports, notably to the *Leviathan*, which, painted by an English camoufleur, Wilkinson, fairly revels in color designed to confuse the eyes of those who would attack her. A great deal has been written about land camouflage, but not so much about the same art as practised on ships. Originally, the purpose was the same—concealment and general low visibility—at least it was so far as the Americans were concerned. The British, on the other hand, employed camouflage with a view to distorting objects and fatiguing the eye, thus seriously affecting range-finding. The British system was known as the "dazzle system," and was opposed to the American idea of so painting a vessel as to cause it to merge into its background.

The American camouflage is based on scientific principles which embody so much in the way of chromatic paradox as to warrant setting forth rather fully, even though at the present time, for good and sufficient reasons relating to German methods of locating vessels, the Americans have more or less abandoned their ideas of low visibility and taken up with the dazzle idea.

A mural painter of New York, William Andrew Mackay, who had long experimented in the chemistry of color (he is now a member of the staff of navy camoufleurs), had applied a process of low visibility to naval vessels long before war broke out in Europe. The basis of his theory of camouflage was that red, green, and violet, in terms of light, make gray; they don't in pigment.

The Mackay scheme of invisibility will be easily grasped by the reader if we take the ex-

RED, GREEN, AND VIOLET 219

ample of the rainbow. The phenomenon of the rainbow, then, teaches us that what we know to be white light, or daylight, is composed of rays of various colors. If an object, say the hull of a vessel at sea, prevents these rays from coming to the eye, that hull, or other object, is of course clearly defined, the reason being that the iron mass shuts out the light-rays behind it. Mr. Mackay discovered that by applying to the sides of a ship paint representing the three light-rays shut out by the vessel's hull—red, green, and violet—the hull is less visible than a similar body painted in solid color.

In a series of experiments made under the supervision of the Navy Department after we entered the war an oil-tanker ship was so successfully painted in imitation of the color-rays of light that, at three miles, the tanker seemed to melt into the horizon. The effect was noted in the morning, at noon, and in the evening. In the case of various big liners, more than 500 feet long, no accurate range could be made for shelling at from three to five miles—the usual shelling distance—while at eight miles the vessels melted into the ocean-mists.

But the first trials of the system were conducted at Newport, in 1913, in conjunction with Lieutenant Kenneth Whiting, of the submarine flotilla. After a period experiments were continued at the Brooklyn Navy Yard. In 1915 Commander J. O. Fisher, U. S. N., painted the periscope of his submarine—the K-6—with the colors of the spectrum. Mr. Mackay got in touch with this officer and explained the work he had done with Lieutenant Whiting. Fisher, deeply interested, invited the painter to deliver a series of lectures to the officers of the submarine flotilla at the Brooklyn Navy Yard.

With the aid of a Maxwell disk—a wheel upon which colored cardboard is placed and then revolved—he demonstrated the difference between paint and light, as set forth in a book on the chemistry of color by the late Ogden N. Rood, of Columbia. He showed, for example, that yellow and blue in light make white, while yellow and blue in pigment make green. The bird colored blue and yellow will be a dull gray at a distance of 100 feet, and will blend perfectly against the dull gray of a tree-trunk at, perhaps, a less distance. The parrot of red, green, and

LOW VISIBILITY

violet plumage turns gray at 100 feet or more, the eye at that distance losing the ability to separate the three color-sensations.

It is upon this principle, then, that ships painted in several varieties of tints and shades form combinations under different lights that cause them to waver and melt into the sea and sky. They *seem* to melt, to be more explicit, because the craft so painted is surrounded by tints and shades that are similar to those employed in painting the craft.

Vessels thus painted, as seen at their docks, present a curious aspect. At their water-lines, and running upward for perhaps twenty feet, are green wave-lines, and above, a dappled effect of red, green, and violet, which involve not only the upper portions of the hull, but the life-boats, masts, and funnels.

This, then, as said, was the American idea as first applied by Mr. Mackay, and which would have been greatly amplified had not listening devices been so perfected as to render it unnecessary for the Germans to see until their quarry was so near, say a mile or two, that no expedient in the way of low visibility would serve. It was then that our navy, which had been following experiments in camouflage, accepted the dazzle system for some of its transports, while retaining the leaden war-paint for other transports and for fighting craft.

The dazzle system as applied on the *Leviathan* and other vessels under jurisdiction of the navy, has for its idea the disruption of outline and deception as to the true course a vessel is following. The writer saw the *Leviathan* under way shortly after she was camouflaged, and at a distance of two miles it was utterly impossible to tell whether she was coming or going; and the observer could not tell whether she had three funnels or six, or only one. It was noted that as her distance from the observer became greater the vessel assumed a variety of effects. Once it seemed as though both bow and stern had dropped off, and finally the big craft suggested in the morning haze nothing so much as a cathedral set in the middle of the bay.

Effects of this sort are produced by vertical stripes of black and white at bow and stern, by long, horizontal lines of black and blue, and by patches of various hues. One funnel is

ZIGZAG COURSES

gray, another blue and white, another all blue. There can be no question that the sum total of effect offends the eye and dazes the senses. Submarines have been known to make errors of eight degrees in delivering torpedoes at dazzle boats even at close range.

In addition to camouflage experiments on one of our great inland lakes, the Navy Department also investigated other ideas relating to the self-protection of craft at sea. Among these was a device by which a vessel zigzags automatically as she proceeds on her ocean course. The advantage of such an invention when the war zone is filled with submarines waiting for a chance for pot shots at craft is obvious.

The Navy Department, in short, has neglected nothing that would tend to enhance the safety of our ships on the sea, and many valuable schemes have been applied. But when all is said and done these defensive elements are and, it seems, must remain subsidiary to the protection as applied from without, the protection of swift destroyers with their depth-bombs, their great speed, and their ability quickly to manœuvre.

CHAPTER XII

THE NAVAL FLYING CORPS—WHAT THE NAVY DEPARTMENT HAS ACCOMPLISHED AND IS ACCOMPLISHING IN THE WAY OF AIR-FIGHTING—EXPERIENCE OF A NAVAL ENSIGN ADRIFT IN THE ENGLISH CHANNEL—SEAPLANES AND FLYING BOATS—SCHOOLS OF INSTRUCTION—INSTANCES OF HEROISM

IN writing of aviation in the navy an incident which befell one of our naval airmen in the English Channel seems to demand primary consideration, not alone because of the dramatic nature of the event, but because it sets forth clearly the nature of the work upon which our flying men of the navy entered as soon as the United States took hostile action against Germany. Our navy aviators, in fact, were the first force of American fighters to land upon European soil after war was declared. Here is the story as told by Ensign E. A. Stone, United States Naval Reserve, after he was rescued from the Channel, where with a companion he had clung for eighty hours without food and drink to the under-side of a capsized seaplane pontoon.

"I left our station in a British seaplane as

IN THE CHANNEL 225

pilot, with Sublieutenant Moore of the Royal Naval Air Service as observer, at 9 o'clock in the morning. Our duty was to convoy patrols. When two hours out, having met our ships coming from the westward, we thought we sighted a periscope ahead, and turned off in pursuit. We lost our course. Our engine dropped dead, and at 11.30 o'clock forced us to land on the surface of a rough sea. We had no kite nor radio to call for assistance, so we released our two carrier-pigeons. We tied a message with our position and the word 'Sinking' on each. The first, the blue-barred one, flew straight off and reached home. But the other, which was white-checked, lit on our machine and would not budge until Moore threw our navigation clock at him, which probably upset him so that he failed us.

"Heavy seas smashed our tail-planes, which kept settling. I saw that they were pulling the machine down by the rear, turning her over. We tore the tail-fabric to lessen the impact of the waves. It wasn't any use. The tail-flat was smashed and its box filled with water.

"This increased the downward leverage and

raised her perpendicularly in the air. At 2.30 P. M. we capsized. We climbed up the nose and 'over the top' to the under-side of the pontoons. Our emergency ration had been in the observer's seat at the back, but we had been so busy trying to repair the motor and save ourselves from turning over that we didn't remember this until too late. When I crawled aft for food Moore saw that I was only helping the machine to capsize. He yelled to me to come back and I did, just in time to save myself from being carried down with the tail and drowned.

"From then on for nearly four days, until picked up by a trawler, we were continually soaked and lashed by seas, and with nothing to eat or drink. We had nothing to cling to, and so to keep from being washed overboard we got upon the same pontoon and hugged our arms about each other's bodies for the whole time. We suffered from thirst. I had a craving for canned peaches. Twice a drizzle came on, wetting the pontoon. We turned on our stomachs and lapped up the moisture, but the paint came off, with salt, and nauseated us. Our limbs grew numb. From time to time the wreckage from torpedoed ships would pass. Two full biscuit-tins came close enough to swim for, but by then in our weakened state we knew that we would drown if we tried to get them. We did haul in a third tin and broke it open; it was filled with tobacco.

"Every day we saw convoys in the distance and vainly waved our handkerchiefs. We had no signal-lights to use at night. Our watches stopped, and we lost all track of time. We realized how easy it was for a submarine out there to escape being spotted. On Sunday night we spied a masthead light and shouted. The ship heard and began to circle us. We saw her port light. Then when the crew were visible on the deck of the vessel, she suddenly put out her lights and turned away.

"'She thinks we are Huns,' said Moore.

"'I hope she does,' said I. 'Then they'll send patrol-boats out to get us. We couldn't be worse off if we were Germans.'

"But no rescue came. The next afternoon a seaplane came from the east. It was flying only 800 feet overhead, aiming down the Channel. It seemed impossible that she could not sight us for the air was perfectly clear. She passed straight above without making any signal, flew two miles beyond, and then came back on her course.

"'Her observer must be sending wireless about us,' I said.

"'Yes, that is why we get no recognition,' said Moore, 'and now she's decided to go back and report.'

"But that plane hadn't even seen us. Our spirits fell. We had been afraid of two things, being picked up by a neutral and interned, or captured by an enemy submarine. Now we even hoped that the enemy—that anything—would get us, to end it all.

"We sighted a trawler about 6 P. M. on Tuesday. She had been chasing a submarine, and so did not seem to take us very seriously at first. We waved at her half an hour before she changed her course. We were both too weak to stand up and signal. We could only rise on our knees. Moore's hands were too swollen to hold a handkerchief, but I had kept my gloves on and was able to do so. The trawler moved warily around us, but finally threw a life-preserver at the end of a line. I yelled that we were too weak to grasp it. She finally hove to, lowered a boat, and lifted us aboard. Then we collapsed.

"I remember asking for a drink and getting water. The skipper would let us take only sips, but he left a bottle alongside me and I drained it. He gave us biscuits, but we couldn't chew or swallow them. We felt no pain until our clothing was ripped off and blood rushed into our swollen legs and arms. Moore lost six toes from gangrene in the hospital. My feet turned black, but decay did not set in."

When the pigeon released by Stone and Moore returned to the base every machine from that seaplane-station, as well as from a station on the French coast, was sent out to search for the missing seaplane, while destroyers and patrol-vessels were notified to be on the lookout. Which shows, after all, how difficult the job of detecting such small objects as submarines is. Stone had enlisted as a seaman, and was trained in aviation. On December 11, 1917, he was detached from the air-station at Hampton Roads and ordered to France for duty, arriving there January 21, 1918. In February he was ordered to report to the commander of the United States naval forces at London for patrol duty in England.

Which shows the way the Navy Department worked in with the French and British Admiralties, using either our own planes or those of our allies.

When the navy's plans concerning the American Naval Flying Corps are completed, it will have an air service of fully 125,000 men, of which 10,000 will be aviators. There will be 10 ground men for every aviator. Observers, inspectors and specialists of various sorts will fill out the total. These seaplanes are of immense value in the war zones. They leave bases for regular patrol duty, watching the ocean carefully, and locating submersibles at a great height. Once a submarine is thus located the seaplane descends to the surface and notifies vessels of the patrol-fleet of the location of the craft, or in cases when the undersea craft is on or near the surface, the aviator will drop bombs upon the vessel. Seaplanes are also sent from the decks of naval vessels to scout the waters through which a fleet may be travelling, while large vessels serving as parentships for the smaller seaplanes—from which they fly and to which they return—ply the infested waters. The service is a valuable one, and a thrilling one, and only the best types of men were selected by the Navy Department to engage in it.

In 1917 Congress appropriated $67,733,000 for aviation for the navy, a sum which permitted the department to proceed on an extensive scale. And right here it may be said that the navy has fared much better than the army in the progressive development of air service. Within a year the flying personnel of the navy had grown to be twenty times greater than it was when we went to war, and where a year ago we had one training-school, we now have forty naval aviation-schools.

The navy has not only strained every nerve to turn out aviators and to produce airplanes, but the development of improved types of planes has not been overlooked, and we now have abroad several fine types of seaplane as well as airplane. The seaplane is merely an airplane with pontoons. It starts from the ground or from the deck of a vessel.

Then there is the flying-boat, developed under naval auspices. This boat takes wing from the water, and is regarded as the most desirable form of aircraft for sea purposes. It is a triumphant instance of our ingenuity, and is built in two sizes, both effective under the peculiar conditions which may dictate the use either of one or the other. The navy has also developed a catapult arrangement for launching seaplanes from the decks of war-ships. This is a moving wooden platform, carrying the seaplane, which runs along a track over the ship's deck. The platform drops into the sea, and the seaplane proceeds on its course through the air.

The progress of the navy was so great in arranging for the home coast-defense aerial service that Secretary Daniels agreed to establish air coast-patrol stations in Europe, and it was not long before our naval aviators were rendering signal service both along the French and the British coasts. There is the understanding that the United States has already

NAVY FACTORIES

taken the lead in naval aviation, not in quantity, to be sure, but in quality and efficiency, as to which the presence of foreign experts studying our new improvements may be regarded as confirmatory evidence.

The Navy Department now has an aircraft factory of its own at Philadelphia, and there flying-boats are now being turned out. Also, five private plants throughout the country are working on navy aircraft exclusively.

The Aircraft Board, which succeeded the Aircraft Production Board, is made up in three parts: a third from the navy, a third from the army, and a third civilian. This board is under the joint direction of the Secretaries of War and the Navy.

The naval flying-schools are located at Pensacola, Fla., Miami, Fla., Hampton Roads, Va., Bay Shore, L. I., and San Diego, Cal. Some of the aviators are drawn from the regular naval forces, but the great majority are of the reserves, young men from civil life, college men and the like, who have the physical qualifications and the nerve to fly and fight above tumultuous waters.

The men training in the naval aviation-schools are enrolled as Second Class Seamen in the Coast Defense Reserve. Their status is similar to that of the midshipmen at Annapolis. Surviving the arduous course of training, they receive commissions as ensigns; if they do not survive they are honorably discharged, being free, of course, to enlist in other branches of service. The courses last about six months, the first period of study being in a ground school, where the cadets study navigation, rigging, gunnery, and other technical naval subjects. Thence the pupil goes to a flight-school, where he learns to pilot a machine. Here, if he comes through, the young cadet is commissioned as an ensign L. All pilots in the Naval Reserve Flying Corps hold commissions, but not all of the pilots in the regular navy are commissioned officers, a few rating as chief petty officers.

The men who act as observers—who accompany the pilots on their trips, taking photographs, dropping bombs and the like—are not commissioned. They are selected from men already in the service, regular seamen, marines, reserves, or volunteers. Of course, these men

ENSIGN READ 235

have their opportunities of becoming pilots. The United States seaplanes carry extremely destructive weapons, which will not be described until after the war. The Germans, it may be assumed, know something about them.

The spirit of our naval pilots, both students and qualified graduates, is of the highest, and foreign naval officers have been quick to express their appreciation of their services. When Ensign Curtis Read was shot down in February, 1918, while flying over the French coast, his funeral was attended by many British army and navy officers, and by representatives of both branches of the French service. Besides the company of American sailors there were squads of French and British seamen, who marched in honor of the young officer. The city of Dunkirk presented a beautiful wreath of flowers.

"Nothing," wrote Ensign Artemus Gates, captain-elect of Yale's 1917 football eleven, and a comrade of Read's in France, to the young officer's mother, "could be more impressive than to see a French general, an admiral,

British staff-officers, and many other officers of the two nations paying homage."

The death of Ensign Stephen Potter, who was killed in a battle with seven German airplanes in the North Sea on April 25, 1918, followed a glorious fight which will live in our naval annals. Potter was the first of our naval pilots to bring down a German airplane, and indeed may have been the first American, fighting under the United States flag, to do this. His triumph was attained on March 19, 1918. Between that time and his death he had engaged in several fights against German airmen, causing them to flee.

And in this country our course of training has been marked by many notable examples of heroism and devotion, none more so than the act of Ensign Walker Weed, who, after his plane had fallen in flames at Cape May, N. J., and he had got loose from his seat and was safe, returned to the burning machine and worked amid the flames until he had rescued a cadet who was pinned in the wreckage. It cost Weed his life, and the man he rescued died after lingering some days; but the act is none the

Copyright by Committee on Public Information.

Scene at an aviation station somewhere in America, showing fifteen seaplanes on beach departing and arriving.

less glorious because the gallant young officer gave his life in vain.

Related to the aviation service, to the extent at least that they observe from an aerial post, are the balloon men of the navy, officers who go aloft with great gas-bags, which, when not in use, are carried on the decks of the larger war-ships engaged in work. From the baskets of these sausage-shaped balloons the observers, armed with telescopes and binoculars, the ocean and the ships of the convoy lying like a map below, sweep the surface of the water for lurking submarines and enemy raiders. The balloons are attached to the war-ships, and are towed along through the air. Just how effective this expedient is, is known only to the Navy Department, but the fact that it is retained argues for its usefulness.

Convoyed merchant vessels steam in a wedge or V-shaped formation. At the apex is a destroyer, following which is an armored cruiser of the *Colorado* or *Tennessee* type. Astern of the cruiser is another destroyer, which tows the captive balloon at the end of a very light but strong steel wire. This balloon-towing destroyer really forms the point of the wedge formation. Behind it are placed the two diverging lines of merchant ships, which follow one another, not bow to stern, but in a sort of echelon position. Down through the centre of the wedge is a line of armed trawlers, while armed vessels steam outside the V. Somewhat astern of the convoy is another destroyer, which tows another captive balloon. As a final means of protection, destroyers fly about on each wing of the convoy.

CHAPTER XIII

ORGANIZATION OF THE NAVAL RESERVE CLASSES—TAKING OVER OF YACHTS FOR NAVAL SERVICE—WORK AMONG THE RESERVES STATIONED AT VARIOUS NAVAL CENTRES—WALTER CAMP'S ACHIEVEMENT

IN expanding the navy to meet war conditions, the regular personnel was increased, naval militia units of various States were taken into the service under the classification National Naval Volunteers, and volunteers were accepted in the following classes: *Fleet Naval Reserve*, made up of those who had received naval training and had volunteered for four years. *Naval Auxiliary Reserve*, made up of seafaring men who had had experience on merchant ships. *Naval Coast Defense Reserve*, made up of citizens of the United States whose technical and practical education made them fitted for navy-yard work, patrol, and the like. *Volunteer Naval Reserve*, made up of men who had volunteered, bringing into service their own boats. And finally, the *Naval Reserve Flying Corps*.

It is from these classes that have come the men to put our navy on a war footing; for while the reserve classifications brought thousands and hundreds of thousands of men into the service, the permanent enlisted strength was kept at the specified figure, 87,000, until last June, when Congress increased the allowance to 131,-485. This action was regarded as one of the most important taken since the country entered the war, inasmuch as it gave notice to the world that the United States in the future intends to have a fleet that will measure up to her prominent position in the world's affairs. It means, too, that the number of commissioned officers would be increased from 3,700, as at present arranged, to some 5,500, which will no doubt mean an opportunity for officers who are now in war service in the various reserve organizations.

When we entered the war, a decision to send a number of our destroyers to France imposed upon the Navy Department the necessity of protecting our own coast from possible submarine attack. We had retained destroyers in this country, of course, and our battle and

NAVAL DISTRICTS

cruiser fleet was here; but a large number of mosquito craft, submarine-chasers, patrol-boats, and the like were urgently demanded. Several hundred fine yachts were offered to the Navy Department under various conditions, and in the Third (New York) District alone some 350 pleasure craft adapted for conversion into war-vessels, were taken over. Some of these were sent overseas to join the patrol-fleet, more were kept here. Besides being used for patrol-work, yachts were wanted for mine-sweepers, harbor patrol-boats, despatch-boats, mine-layers, and parent-ships. They were and are manned almost exclusively by the Naval Reserves, and operated along the Atlantic coast under the direction of officers commanding the following districts: First Naval District, Boston; Second Naval District, Newport, R. I.; Third Naval District, New York City; Fourth Naval District, Philadelphia; Fifth Naval District, Norfolk, Va.

Hundreds of sailors, fishermen, seafaring men generally, and yachtsmen joined the Naval Coast Defense Reserve, which proved to be an extremely popular branch of the service with college men. Most of the reserves of this class —there were nearly 40,000 of them—were required for the coast-patrol fleet, and they had enlisted for service in home waters. But when the need for oversea service arose the reserves made no objection at all to manning transports and doing duty on patrol, mine-laying, minesweeping, and other craft engaged in duty in the war zone.

In the course of taking over yachts by the Navy Department, Franklin D. Roosevelt, who has been so efficient and untiring in his capacity as Assistant Secretary of the Navy, charged that yachtsmen were not helping the government, and were holding their craft for high prices. Probably this was the case in enough instances to make Mr. Roosevelt impatient, but it would seem that the large body of yacht-owners did their best, not only donating their yachts to the government or selling them at a fair price, but by themselves enlisting in the service.

There were yachtsmen who, in addition to giving their boats, defrayed the cost of maintenance. Great craft such as G. W. C. Drexel's *Alcedo* (already noted as sunk by a torpedo),

A. Curtiss James's *Aloha*, J. C. and A. N. Brady's *Atlantic*, A. C. Burrage's *Aztec*, I. T. Bush's *Christabel*, H. A. Loughlin's *Corona*, J. P. Morgan's *Corsair*, Robert T. Graves's *Emeline*, E. P. and J. W. Alker's *Florence*, Edgar Palmer's *Guinevere*, George F. Baker, Jr.'s *Wacouta*, W. L. Harkness's *Cythera*, Robert Goelet's *Nahma*, J. G. Bennett's *Lysistrata*, John Borden's *Kanawha*, Henry Walter's *Narada*, Howard Gould's *Niagara*, Horace G. Dodge's *Nokomis*, Vincent Astor's *Noma*, Mrs. E. H. Harriman's *Sultana*, Morton F. Plant's *Vanadis*, P. W. Rouss's *Winchester*, *Aphrodite*, the O. H. Payne estate; F. G. Bourne's *Alberta*, and Edward Harkness's *Wakiva*—these great yachts among other steam-driven palaces, passed into the hands of the Navy Department in one way or another, and have performed valiant service. Some of them, indeed, have ended their careers violently in service.

The government ripped out the costly interiors and converted these panelled floating abodes of the wealthy into serviceable fighters, and no doubt will retain those that survive when the war is ended. There were instances where the owners of yachts and the Navy Department could not agree on prices to be paid. The naval authorities finally suggested that the owners should name one representative, and the Navy Department another, and terms thus agreed upon. It was not, however, until the Department appointed a special board, whose duty was to secure suitable boats without further delay, that affairs began to proceed smoothly. The first move was to have the International Mercantile Marine Company's shipping experts act as agents of the special board, and from that time on there was no further trouble.

The Mercantile Marine experts not only brought about the transfer of yachts to the navy, but superintended alterations above and below deck, arming, outfitting, coaling, painting, and provisioning the converted war-ships. While this was in progress the Navy Department was having built a fleet of submarine-chasers of the 110-foot class, which, together with the yachts taken over, offered abundant opportunities for oversea service, which the sailors enrolled in the Coast Defense Division were not slow to accept after they were requested

From a photograph copyright by International Film Service.

Captain's inspection at Naval Training Station, Newport, R. I.

to transfer their enrolment from Class 4 to Class 2, under which classification they were eligible to be sent abroad. Thus thousands of young men who had enlisted for coast-patrol duty, were sent aboard transports, submarine-chasers, and war-ships generally, for service in the European war zones.

And with this constant outflow of trained men from the various naval training-stations of the country, the influx of newly enlisted reserves into these schools gives assurance that the Navy Department will never be embarrassed for lack of material wherewith to man its boats. And there is the likelihood that as our new merchant vessels are launched and put into commission, they will be manned by reserves from the navy training-schools with officers furnished by the Deck School at Pelham Bay and the Engineers' School at Hoboken. The government, of course, is in complete control of the merchant marine; but in our present condition many American ships have to be manned by aliens. It will be surprising if this state of affairs will not be corrected as swiftly as the Navy Department is able to do so, and thus we may expect to see our young seamen diverted in ever-increasing numbers to merchant vessels, the precise degree, of course, to be dependent upon the needs of the fighting vessels. Young officers, no doubt, will receive commands, and in general a thriving mercantile marine will be in readiness for operation when war ends.

Our naval training-stations are models of businesslike precision and well-ordered proficiency. Herein are taught everything from bread-baking and cooking to engineering, gunnery, and other maritime accomplishments. Long before we had entered the war a determination had been reached by individuals and organizations external to the Navy—and Army—Departments, to bring to the naval stations as many and as complete comforts and conveniences of civilization as possible.

Almost immediately after the American declaration of war, the purposes of the authors of this scheme were presented to Congress, and permission for them to carry out their mission was given through the formation of the sister commissions, the Army and the Navy Commissions on Training Camp Activities.

WALTER CAMP

Although entirely separate in their work—one dealing entirely with the men in the army, the other with those in the navy camps—the same authority on organized humanitarian effort, Raymond B. Fosdick of New York City, one of the original group with whom the plan originated, was chosen chairman of both. Each commission's work was divided among departments or subcommissions.

In the Navy Commission, one group, the Library Department, supplied the enlisted men of the navy stations, as far as possible, with books, another with lectures, another with music, vocal and instrumental, another with theatrical entertainments, including moving-pictures, and another subcommission directed the recreational sport.

Mr. Walter Camp, for thirty years the moving spirit, organizer, adviser, and athletic strategist of Yale, was chosen chairman of the Athletic Department, with the title General Commissioner of Athletics for the United States Navy.

Taking up his task in midsummer, 1917, three months after declaration of war by the United States, Mr. Camp at once brought his ability, experience, and versatility into play in organizing recreational sport in the navy stations. By this time every naval district was fast filling with its quota of enlisted men, and the plan of the Navy Department to place an even hundred thousand men in the stations before the close of the year was well along toward completion.

Swept from college, counting-room, professional office, and factory, often from homes of luxury and elegance, to the naval stations, where, in many cases arrangements to house them were far from complete, the young men of the navy found themselves surrounded by conditions to which they pluckily and patiently reconciled themselves, but which could not do otherwise than provoke restlessness and discomfort.

Under these conditions the work of the Navy Commission was particularly timely and important, and that of Mr. Camp was of conspicuous value through the physical training and mental stimulus which it provided for patriotic, yet half homesick young Americans, from whom not only material comfort and luxury, but en-

ATHLETICS

tertainment of all kinds, including recreational sport, had been taken.

Mr. Camp defined the scope of the Athletic Department of the Commission as follows, in taking up his duties:

"Our problem is to provide athletics for the men in order to duplicate as nearly as possible the home environment, produce physical fitness with high vitality, and in this we feel that we shall have the most generous and whole-souled co-operation from the Y. M. C. A., the Knights of Columbus, the War Camp Community Service, and all the agencies that are established in and about the camps."

Launching the movement to "duplicate home conditions" in recreational sport, Mr. Camp appointed athletic directors in the largest districts during the fall, and in every one the programme of seasonal sport was carried out, comparable in extent and quality with that which every enlisted man in the stations would have enjoyed as participant or spectator in his native city or town, school or college, had he not entered military service.

The athletic directors who were chosen were,

in every case, experienced organizers of all-round sports, and several of them were former college coaches or star athletes. In the First District at Boston, George V. Brown, for thirteen years athletic organizer for the Boston Athletic Association, was named; in the Second, at Newport, Doctor William T. Bull, the former Yale football coach and medical examiner; in the Third, Frank S. Bergin, a former Princeton football-player; in the Fourth, at League Island, Franklin T. McCracken, an athletic organizer of Philadelphia; and at the Cape May Station Harry T. McGrath, of Philadelphia, an all-round athlete.

In the Fifth District, Doctor Charles M. Wharton, of Philadelphia, a prominent neurologist and University of Pennsylvania football coach, took charge late in the fall, resigning in April, 1918, to become field-secretary of the Navy Commission on Training Camp Activities. and being succeeded by Louis A. Young, of Philadelphia, a former University of Pennsylvania football-player, captain, and all-round athlete.

In the Sixth District, at Charleston, S. C.,

SPORTS DIRECTORS

Walter D. Powell, a former University of Wisconsin football-player, and later athletic director at Western Reserve University, was placed in charge of the programme, and at the Great Lakes Station, Herman P. Olcott, who had been football coach at Yale and athletic director at the University of Kansas, began his work in October.

Arthur C. Woodward, formerly interscholastic athletic organizer in Washington, was placed in charge of the Puget Sound Station in Bremerton; and Elmer C. Henderson, athletic director in Seattle high schools, was appointed to the Seattle Station.

David J. Yates, of New York City, an all-round athlete and athletic supervisor, was appointed director at Pensacola, combining the work of athletic organization with the physical training of the aviators in that station.

Intensely practical and stimulating as well as picturesque and almost fascinating programmes in their attractiveness were carried out during the fall at the larger stations. The Newport football eleven, captained by "Cupid" Black, the former Yale gridiron star, and containing such all-American players as Schlachter, of Syracuse; Hite, of Kentucky; Barrett, of Cornell; and Gerrish, of Dartmouth; the Boston team, including in its membership Casey, Enright, and Murray, of Harvard; the League Island eleven, captained by Eddie Mahan, the former Harvard all-round player; and the Great Lakes team, largely composed of representative Western gridiron stars, played a series of games on the fields of the East and the Middle West, which lifted, temporarily, the curtain which seemed to have fallen on the college football heroes when they passed into naval service, and allowed the sport-loving public of America to again see them in athletic action.

During the winter the value of the athletic department of the Commission on Training-Camp Activities to the Navy became clearer as the indoor programmes, which were organized by Commissioner Camp and his lieutenants, the athletic directors, were carried out. Boxing, wrestling, swimming, hockey, basket-ball, and other athletic instructors were appointed to develop every kind of indoor sport until there were no nights when, in the large auditoriums of the navy stations, some programme of winter sport was not being given for the entertainment of the thousands of young men in camp. Mass sports were favored, the general rule being laid down that the chief value of every game lay in accordance with its ability to attract a larger or a smaller number of participants or spectators.

Among the sports which were tried, boxing proved its value as the chief. Attracting crowds limited only by the size of the auditoriums, the boxing-bouts which were held, usually semiweekly in all the stations, were a most diverting feature of winter life in camp. One reason for their popularity can be directly traced to their enforced use in the physical training of the stations. Lending themselves ideally to mass instruction, the boxing exercises were taught to classes usually numbering between 150 and 200 persons, and the fact that every marine studied boxing contributed to the size and the interest of the crowds that packed the ringsides at the frequent bouts.

The teaching of boxing was also emphasized for its life-saving value in a military sense.

The maxim is taught that "every move of the boxer is a corresponding move by the bayonet-fighter." Thus, the "jab" corresponds to the "lunge," and the "counter" to the "parry." To illustrate this boxing instruction, and to apply it to bayonet-drill, a set of admirable moving-pictures was made, such clever pugilists as Johnnie Kilbane, Bennie Leonard, Kid McCoy, and Jim Corbett posing for the boxing, and Captain Donovan, the eminent English bayonet instructor, for the bayonet films, which were exhibited for instruction purposes in every navy station. Boxing tournaments, station championships, and army-navy championship bouts were given with crowded houses everywhere.

Early in the winter Commissioner Camp gave directions for standardized sets of instruction in both boxing and wrestling, and as a result, in every camp in the country the groups of navy men were taught the same methods of rudimentary boxing for their value in a military sense, as well as their value as recreational sports.

Soon after the thousands of young men began

SWIMMING

gathering in the navy camps, the discovery was made that not half the number was able to swim. For men destined for sea life, this was a vital handicap, and early in the spring of 1918 a campaign was launched to increase the number of swimming instructors and the facilities which were available for the instruction of the young men both in sea and river, as well as in pools and tanks, and it was decided to hold station tournaments, races, and all varieties of swimming events during the season, in conjunction with such individual instruction as it was necessary to give novices in the art of swimming.

Rowing was developed during the season of 1918 to the extent which was made possible by the presence of cutters in the different stations. Wherever possible, crews were coached in the rudiments of rowing by old oarsmen. Racing between the cutter crews in whatever station was ordered for every available date, and sometimes as many as twenty boats were lined up abreast, and were shot away for the brushes between the cutter crews in some of the larger stations, furnishing a variety of sport comparable only with the brilliant scenes at the intercollegiate races over the Thames course at New London, or the Hudson at Poughkeepsie.

As football reigned supreme in the fall programme of recreational sport, and boxing in the winter, baseball furnished the greatest solace for the men of the navy marooned from city and college games. Scattered through the stations were former major and minor league and college players in abundance, and nines, vying in their intrinsic strength with major-league champions, were organized in every station. Jack Barry in the Boston District, "Toots" Schultz in the Newport, Phil Choinard in the Great Lakes, Davy Robertson in the Norfolk, Jack Hoey in the Charleston, and Paul Strand in the Seattle Districts, were a few of the stars of national reputation who headed the teams. More valuable, however, to the true purpose of the organization of recreational sports than the individual stars and the district teams were the leagues which were formed in the respective stations, for they kept every naval base engrossed in a wholesome athletic interest, and furnished natural relaxation from the exacting drill and drudgery of every-day routine.

TRACK ATHLETICS

Track athletic stars of college and amateur athletic organizations were scattered through every station, and the organization of track meets was begun as soon as the men of the navy reached the camps. In October, 1917, before some 15,000 people, the track men of the Boston Station took part in games on Boston Common, a track carnival was held in the Harvard Stadium a month later, and in every station of the country track tournaments were held during the season of 1918.

For April 19, the anniversary of the battle of Lexington, a patriotic team relay race was ordered for every station in the country by Commissioner Camp. In the First District the route lay over the historic Marathon course from Ashland into Boston, and most of the teams represented either the army cantonment at Camp Devens or the First Naval District. In most instances the races were run from an army to a navy camp, messages being carried from the commanding officer in one to the similar officer in the other. Secretary Daniels of the navy witnessed the First District event.

In most cases the races were conducted as a feature and auxiliary in the Third Liberty Loan campaign, which was nearing its height, and proved a valuable factor in promoting the success of the drive. It is believed that this is the first national race which was ever held in every section of the United States at the request of one individual, and it was appropriate that the first of a series of such athletic events should be of a purely patriotic scope and a part of the national military service.

Closely related to the work of Commissioner Camp in the naval stations was his successful attempt to secure for the aviators the use of skilful flight surgeons and college trainers to safeguard the physical condition of the airmen. At the annual conference of the National Collegiate Association, which was held in New York City in December, 1917, Mr. Camp called attention to the fact that the conditioning of the aviators was similar to that of college athletes, and was just as vital; and, inasmuch as the physical safety of football-players and other college athletic contestants was successfully guaranteed by experienced trainers, he recommended that several of the best be selected from

TRAINERS FOR FLIERS

leading American universities to go to the aviation-fields and take charge of the conditioning of the fliers. Two months later, recommendation was made by the aviation department that from ten to fifteen such trainers be named by Mr. Camp to go at once to the aviation-stations and pass judgment on the condition of the fliers before they were allowed to leave the ground. An unusually large number of deaths took place in the United States during practise flights of the aviators early in the spring of 1918, and in May the government authorized the appointment of an adequate number of college trainers to carry out the work of conditioning the airmen. Before this time reports of conditions in England and France established the fact that more deaths of aviators had been caused by the flight of the airmen when in poor physical condition than by any defect in the flying-machine.

In all, Mr. Camp's work has been adequately recognized by the Navy Department as of the greatest benefit, and the constant stream of testimony from the reserve seamen attached to the various stations that "there is no place like the navy," is, in some part due to the activities of this veteran Yale athlete and his associates.

CHAPTER XIV

THE UNITED STATES MARINE CORPS—FIRST MILITARY BRANCH OF THE NATIONAL SERVICE TO BE SANCTIONED BY CONGRESS—LEAVING FOR THE WAR—SERVICE OF THE MARINES IN VARIOUS PARTS OF THE GLOBE—DETAILS OF EXPANSION OF CORPS—THEIR PRESENT SERVICE ALL OVER THE WORLD

WHEN orders came for some 2,700 United States marines to go to France there was little circumstance, or general fuss and feathers, at the League Island Navy Yard, in Philadelphia. The Marine Corps, which is under control of the Navy Department, was quite used to such things. Through all the years when trouble had occurred in our island possessions, in the West Indies, Central America, or where not, it was the marines who received orders to start out and settle things. As a consequence, orders to go to France were merely in the line of the customary day's work.

Thus the only ceremony characterizing the departure of Colonel Charles A. Doyen and his men from the navy-yard at Philadelphia, was a brief speech by Major-General George Barnett, commandant of the corps, to the officers of the field and staff of the overseas outfit, and to the company officers. No colors were unfurled. No reporters or press photographers were present. The regimental bandsmen went to war with their instruments cased and rifles over their shoulders. On the navy-yard parade-ground a sailor baseball nine from one of the battleships was at practice. The marines slipped away so quietly that the ball-players did not know until afterward that they had missed seeing the departure of 2,700 men bound for the battle-front.

At 2.30 o'clock that afternoon the baseball-players had the parade-ground to themselves, and no one was in sight on the street in front of the home of the post commander of marines but a small boy in rompers, playing with a fox-terrier. A few seconds later the head of a column of soldiers of the sea, clad in khaki, and in heavy marching order, swung into that brick-paved street. The major-general commandant and a group of officers from headquarters took up posts on the turf of the parkway beside the curb. A sergeant of marines, in khaki, came running across the parade-ground, set up a motion-picture camera, and began to crank. Another sergeant was snapping "stills," as the column came to a halt and faced about toward the group of officers.

The company officers of the battalion stepped out in front of Major-General Barnett and saluted. Then the general spoke for a few minutes in an every-day, conversational tone. He told the men that he trusted them, that he knew they would uphold the honor and high traditions of the corps when fighting in France under General Pershing. The officers saluted and stepped back to their places. The battalion stood at rigid attention for a moment. Then with a snap, rifles jumped to shoulders, squads swung into column formation, and the line passed swiftly down the street to the gate of the navy-yard.

No cheering crowd greeted the marines as they emerged from the gateway, and only a few persons saw them board a train of day-coaches for a near-by port. The sun-browned fighting men, all veterans of campaigning in Hayti and Santo Domingo, waved their cam-

AT THE NAVY-YARD

paign hats from the windows and the train moved away.

Half an hour later another battalion marched briskly down the same street from the end of a tree-lined vista, and formed on the parade-ground. The bluejacket nine was still at baseball practice, but the marines were at the far end of the field, too distant to attract particular attention. A third battalion formed and stacked arms in front of the barracks. Presently, without so much as a bugle-note for warning, the two battalions formed, picked up their arms, and defiled out of sight, back of a screen of shade-trees.

A quarter of an hour later a rumor came to the bluejacket ball-players that the marines were boarding ship. The jacky beside the home plate dropped his bat and ran toward the street, his team-mates close behind him. They were too late to catch even a glimpse of the rear-guard. The marines, just as swiftly and quietly as if they were on their way to Hayti, Santo Domingo, Vera Cruz, or Nicaragua, had departed.

We all know what they did and what subsequent regiments of marines sent to the front has done. Their fighting in the region of Torcy in the German drive of last June, when the Teutonic shock troops got a reverse shock from the marines, has already become a part of our brightest fighting tradition. The marines are fighters, have always been so—but it took their participation in this war to bring them prominently before the public.

"Who and what are the marines?" was the question frequently asked when the communiques began to retail their exploits. Ideas were very hazy concerning them, and indeed, while we all are by this time quite familiar with what they can do, there are many of us even now who do not quite know what they are.

Be it said, then, that the United States Marine Corps was authorized by the Continental Congress on November 10, 1775, and therefore has the distinction of being the oldest military branch in the United States service. The corps served valiantly throughout the Revolutionary War, and was disbanded at the close of the war, April 11, 1782. But the corps was reorganized and permanently established

DUTIES OF MARINES

July 11, 1798. From that day to this, its officers have been zealous participants in every expedition and action in which the navy has engaged, and in many trying campaigns they have won distinction with their brethren of the army. Their motto is *Semper Fidelis*, and ever have they lived up to it in war and in peace.

The marines serve both on land and sea. They are trained, clothed, and equipped very much as are soldiers of the land forces. In their preliminary instruction on shore, at navy-yards and naval-stations, they are instructed and drilled in the duties of infantry soldiers, field-artillery men, and as machine-gun companies. In preparation for their duties as landing-parties from ships of the navy, for expeditionary duty, and as defenders of naval advance bases, they are further trained in the use of portable search-lights, the wireless telegraph, the heliograph, and the various other methods of signalling. They study range-finding; erection, operation, and maintenance of telegraph and telephone lines; planting of land and submarine mines; handling of torpedoes; erection and demolition of bridges; building of roads; knotting and splicing of ropes; handling of heavy weights; fitting of gun-gear and the various methods of slinging and transporting ordnance, and the mounting in suitable shore positions of guns of 3, 5, and 6 inch caliber.

In their service on battleships and cruisers, the marines form a part of the ship's complement for battle, manning the 6-inch, 5-inch, 3-inch, and 6-pounder guns of the intermediate and secondary batteries. They are trained and fully equipped for instant service as landing-parties for duty on shore.

Great mobility and facilities for quick action are required of the marines, and they must be kept in readiness to move at a moment's notice and be prepared for service in any climate. They have seen service in Egypt, Algiers, Tripoli, Mexico, China, Japan, Korea, Cuba, Porto Rico, Panama, Nicaragua, Santo Domingo, Formosa, Sumatra, Hawaii, Samoa, Guam, Alaska, and the Philippine Islands.

Lieutenant P. N. O'Bannon, of the Marine Corps, hoisted the first American flag ever flown over a fortress of the Old World when Derne, a Tripolitan stronghold, was taken by

"SOLDIERS AND SAILORS, TOO" 267

assault on April 27, 1805. The first regulars who entered the fortress of Chapultepec, in Mexico City, when it was taken by storm on September 13, 1847, were marines, under command of Major Levi Twigg. Under command of Robert E. Lee, later commanding the Confederate Army, marines captured John Brown at Harper's Ferry, in 1859. A battalion of marines under Captain John L. Broome, occupied New Orleans upon its surrender, and hoisted the American flag on the custom house, April 29, 1862. A battalion of marines, 646 officers and men, commanded by Lieutenant-Colonel R. W. Huntington, was the first American force that landed in Cuba in 1898, when it established a base for Admiral Sampson's fleet at Guantanamo, holding their position against Spanish regulars who were said to number 7,000.

The United States Marines of the battleship *Oregon*, Captain John T. Myers commanding, were the first American troops to enter Peking just before the Boxer insurrection broke out in 1900. Lieutenant-Colonel Neville's marines were the first ashore at Vera Cruz in April, 1914.

It will thus be seen that the Marine Corps of the navy is a highly useful organization, and that it has played a large part in carrying our flag to the fore in all our wars. Until 1883 officers in the corps were appointed from civil life. Beginning with that year, all vacancies were filled from graduates of the Naval Academy at Annapolis. This practice continued until 1898, when the increase in the corps was so rapid that the Academy could not furnish a sufficient number of officers. Since then, until 1915, appointments were made from civil life and by promotion from the ranks. In 1915 vacancies again began to be filled from Annapolis, but the entrance of our country into the war brought about the award of commissions on a broader scale. To-day, serving with the marines in France are a number of young officers who, a year or two ago, were well-known college athletes, such men as Eddie Mahan, of Harvard; Billy Moore, of Princeton; Harry LeGore, of Yale; Albert Baston, of Minnesota, and many other gridiron and diamond heroes, who were attracted to this branch of the service by the opportunities offered for quick action.

OFFICERS' SCHOOL

There is a Marine Officers' School at Norfolk, to which young men appointed second lieutenants from civil life are sent for two years' intensive study before being assigned to regular duty. The course covers general subjects, and also all military branches, such as engineering, topography, gunnery, electricity, signalling, torpedo operation, and the like. In the case of college men appointed lieutenants for war service, the majority had just been graduated or were seniors in their respective institutions; as a consequence, little time was lost in the study of general subjects, the idea being to concentrate upon military subjects. In short, the Plattsburg idea was put into effect, with what results may be judged by the words of high praise which have been said concerning the marine subalterns in France.

Since war began the corps has grown from a total of 13,266 enlisted men and 426 officers to a present strength of 38,629 enlisted men and 1,389 officers. The increase in enlisted men has been through voluntary enlistment; in one instance a college battalion enlisted as a whole. The personnel represents all classes of the community: college and business men, athletes, mechanics, laborers, and in one instance a former Congressman, who, although slightly over the usual age, attained the rank of second lieutenant through his devotion to duty and application.

The recruit depots at Port Royal, S. C., and Mare Island, Cal., have proved equal to the demands made upon them, and here the preliminary training of the mass of recruits has been accomplished. No detail of the training of a soldier has been neglected, and on the transfer of these new men to the concentration camp at Quantico, Va., the majority has worn the insignia of expert rifleman, sharpshooter, or marksman. Here at Quantico the men have completed their course of intensive training in the new organizations formed at that post for service overseas. Five regiments of infantry, with their attendant replacement units, have been organized in addition to a brigade of artillery, since the creation of this new post, in June, 1917.

Besides the brigade of marines in France, it is necessary to maintain forces of marines in

From a photograph copyright by International Film Service.

American Marines who took part in the Marne offensive on parade in Paris, July 4, 1918.

FAR-FLUNG SERVICE

Santo Domingo, Hayti, the Virgin Islands, Guam, Cuba, China, the Philippines, Porto Rico, and Honolulu, while there is a small detachment in London. The fleet of battleships and cruisers absorbs a goodly percentage of the present force, while at the same time it has been necessary to supply men to augment the garrisons of the navy-yards, naval ammunition depots, radio-stations, and other posts of the country.

CHAPTER XV

SCOPE OF THE NAVY'S WORK IN VARIOUS PARTICULARS—FOOD—FUEL—NAVAL CONSULTING BOARD—PROJECTILE FACTORY—EXPENDITURES—INCREASE OF PERSONNEL

IN the way of progress in naval construction or appliance, it is not the opinion of our naval technicians that the war from its inception to the present time has developed any hitherto unknown feature. Guns and ships, to be sure, have increased in size, and details of the submarine and airplane have vastly improved these weapons of offense, but substantially no weapon hitherto known has been discredited by use in this war, and even all classes of war-ships built before the war have withstood the test of new conditions as to their usefulness along the lines for which they were originally designed.

Germany has not improved the submarine, except in detail. Undersea craft of that country which have been recently captured show

BATTLESHIPS STILL SUPREME

little deviation from the original lines of the submarine as used in the German Navy four years ago. They are larger—the new ones, that is—but the principle of their construction is fundamental, and the development not unnatural.

Our modern submarine-chasers are merely a modified form of the torpedo-boat destroyer. The depth-bomb was known before it was employed as one of the most effective weapons against the submarine.

Naval authorities join in defending the big battleship which has come into action but little in the course of the war thus far. There is to be considered, however, the moral effect of Great Britain's big fleet, which has maintained control of the seas for four years. Similarly our American fleet is regarded as the first and decisive line of defense on our shores.

Battleships, it is true, do not figure frequently in the official communiques, but none the less they are playing their part. Battleships are absolutely a necessary and vital element to every nation at war. They constitute the last great line of defense, and in this war they have succeeded in keeping the seas practically free of enemy menace save under the water.

In this final chapter may be included various details, facts, and figures which are necessary as giving further point to the enormous scope of the war activities of the Navy Department. In 1916, then, the officers and enlisted men of the regular navy and the Marine Corps totalled 82,738. In March, 1918, the strength of the naval forces, including regular navy, marines, naval reserve force, national naval volunteers, and coast guard, was 349,997, and at this writing is more than 400,000. The total expenditures of the navy from the date of its establishment in 1794 to 1916, inclusive, were $3,367,160,591.77, only about $34,000,000 in excess of the appropriations real and pending since August 26, 1916. For the specific purposes of new construction appropriations totalling $295,000,000 have been made.

On April 1, 1917, there were building 15 battleships, 6 battle cruisers, 7 scout cruisers, 27 destroyers, 61 submarines, 2 fuel ships, 1 supply ship, 1 transport, 1 gunboat, 1 hospital ship, and 1 ammunition ship. Since that date contracts have been placed for 949 vessels, including 100 submarine-chasers for co-belligerent nations. The Board of Construction and Repair has also prepared in co-operation with the Shipping Board, a number of preliminary designs of simplified merchant vessels, varying in length from 400 to 800 feet.

In June of 1917, 180 acres of land were secured at South Charleston, W. Va., for a projectile plant, which is now in operation. An armor-plate factory will be constructed. In one plant manufacturing steel forgings the output was increased 300 per cent within two months after government managers were installed.

The expansion of the naval establishment has necessitated a great increase in facilities for the assembling, housing, and distribution of stores, and these needs have been largely met at Boston, Philadelphia, and Hampton Roads by large emergency and permanent constructions.

In the Commissary Department the effort has been to see that the naval forces continue to be what the surgeon-general has stated they are: the "best fed body of men in the world."

Sailors are no poison squad, and all efforts to try upon the officers and seamen of the force any experimental or test food have been rigorously suppressed. The high cost of living has been reflected in the cost of the navy ration, but the price has been met. There were clothing shortages during the early weeks of the war, but prompt and efficient action by the Bureau of Supplies and Accounts has remedied all this.

Fuel for the navy has been handled by means of allotments placed with the principal operators in coal-producing States, the prices being fixed by the Fuel Administrator. The navy's stocks of fuel have been maintained to capacity, and shipments have been made to the fleet within the time required in all cases. Fuel oil has been obtained in similar manner at the prices fixed by the Federal Trade Commission. The Medical Department of the navy passed quietly from a peace to a war footing on April 6, 1917, and has since continued to give adequate and satisfactory service. With the completion of a hospital ship now building, the navy will have four hospital ships as against one when war began. Prior to the war there were about 375 medical officers on duty. There are to-day 1,675 medical officers in active service, and 200 more on reserve. Where 30 dental surgeons were formerly employed there are now 245. The number of female nurses has increased from 160 to 880.

The President at the outbreak of war directed the Navy Department to take over such radio-stations as might be required for naval communications, all others being closed. Fifty-three commercial radio-stations were thus taken into the Naval Communication Service. Because of duplications, twenty-eight of these stations were closed. Thousands of small amateur radio-stations were closed. At present no radio communication is permitted on United States territory (not including Alaska), except through stations operated by the Navy Communication Department or by the War Department.

With the need of operators apparent, a school for preliminary training in radio-telegraphy was established in each naval district, and when the need for a central final training-school developed, Harvard University offered the use of buildings, laboratories, and dormitories for this purpose.

The offer was accepted, and now the naval-radio school at Harvard is one of the largest educational institutions in the country. There is another final training-school at Mare Island, Cal. The navy supplies the operators for the rapidly increasing number of war vessels, and has undertaken to supply radio operators for all merchant vessels in transatlantic service.

At Harvard and Mare Island the radio students are put through four months' courses, which embraces not only radio-telegraphy and allied subjects, but military training. Some 500,000 men have been undergoing courses at these two schools alone.

When war occurred the Coast Guard was transferred from the Treasury Department to the Navy Department, and the personnel now consists of 227 officers and 4,683 warrant officers and enlisted men.

In the work of examining and considering the great volume of ideas and devices and inventions submitted from the public, the Naval Consulting Board has rendered a signal service. Beginning March, 1917, the Navy Department was overwhelmed with correspondence so great

NAVAL CONSULTING BOARD 279

that it was almost impossible to sort it. Letters, plans, and models were received at the rate of from 5 to 700 a day. Within a year upward of 60,000 letters, many including detailed plans, some accompanied by models, have been examined and acted upon. To do this work a greatly enlarged office force in the Navy Department was necessary, and offices were established in New York and San Francisco. While a comparatively small number of inventions have been adopted—some of them of considerable value—the majority has fallen into the class of having been already known, and either put into use or discarded after practical test.

And thus the Navy Department is carrying on its share of the war, a share significant at the very outset as one of our most important weapons in the establishment of the causes for which the United States entered the great conflict.

CHAPTER XVI

THE BEGINNING OF THE END—REPORTS IN LONDON THAT SUBMARINES WERE WITHDRAWING TO THEIR BASES TO HEAD A BATTLE MOVEMENT ON THE PART OF THE GERMAN FLEET—HOW THE PLAN WAS FOILED—THE SURRENDER OF THE GERMAN FLEET TO THE COMBINED BRITISH AND AMERICAN SQUADRONS—DEPARTURE OF THE AMERICAN SQUADRON—WHAT MIGHT HAVE HAPPENED HAD THE GERMAN VESSELS COME OUT TO FIGHT

IN the early fall of 1918 an American naval officer, who enjoyed to a peculiar degree the confidence of certain officers of the British Admiralty, was attending to duties of an extremely confidential nature in London when one morning he was accosted by a friend, an officer high in the councils of His Majesty's Navy.

"M——," he said, "I have rather an important bit of news. Within a few weeks—in fact, we cannot quite tell how soon—there is going to be the greatest naval engagement the world has ever seen. We are ready for them, though, and we shall win."

The American was naturally curious, and in reply to his questions the Briton went on to say that from certain intelligence quarters word had come that the trend of German U-boats back to their bases—which had been noted for a week or so—contained a grim meaning. It meant, in fine, the emergence of the German fleet, headed by the submarines, prepared for a final battle to establish the question of sea power.

One may imagine the tenseness that reigned at the Admiralty, and the code messages that flew back and forth between London and the flag-ship of the British and American battle fleet. As it happened, the German sea fighters never sallied forth in battle array, their final appearance being less warlike.

But they would have come, it transpired later, had not the sailors of the fleet intercepted messages from German officers to their families, bidding a last good-by. They never expected to return from this last fight. But the seamen were of a different mind from their officers. They declined to go forth to a losing battle, and they struck. This, then, appears to be the reason why the German battleships and armored cruisers and the like did not come forth to battle—at least this is one of the stories told in navy circles.

With the events that followed the cessation of hostilities on November 11 almost every American is familiar. The armistice of that date demanded that Germany give her entire fleet to the keeping of England. For a discussion of the surrender the German light cruiser *Koenigsberg* brought representatives from the Soldiers' and Sailors' Council, which was then in nominal control of the German fleet, into the Firth of Forth. Admiral Beatty refused to deal with these representatives, and insisted that all arrangements be made through some flag-officer of the imperial fleet.

Thereupon Admiral von Reuter, the commanding German officer, went aboard the *Queen Elizabeth*, and there arranged with Admiral Beatty and his flag-officers for the surrender. At dinner the German officers dined at one table, the British at another. After more discussion the *Koenigsberg* departed for Kiel about ten that night. The commander-in-chief then issued an order to all his ships, prescribing the entire details of the surrender.

AMERICAN FLEET JOINS BRITISH 283

The American battle squadron got under way about 4 A. M. November 21, 1918, and steamed from the Forth bridge out of the Firth into the North Sea.

The entire Grand Fleet was here concentrated, formed in two long parallel lines steaming due east six miles apart, our American squadron being the second one in the northern line. By that time the Sixth Battle Squadron was composed of the *New York*, *Texas*, *Wyoming*, *Arkansas*, and *Florida*, the *Delaware* having returned home. Our ships were led by the *New York*. About 9 A. M. the men crowding the decks sighted some smoke coming dead ahead out of the mist, and in a short time the German battle-cruisers were plainly seen leading the other German ships in their last trip at sea under their own flag. They were not flying battle-flags. At this time every one of the Anglo-American ships was at her battle station, turrets were fully manned, and all preparations made for treachery at the last minute.

The German line, led by the *Seydlitz*, steamed slowly between the Allied lines, keeping perfect station, and when their flag-ship came abreast of the *Queen Elizabeth* the signal was given for the whole Grand Fleet to make a turn of 180 degrees, and return into port with the humiliated enemy. The appearance of the enemy ships was very good. There is no doubt they were magnificent fighting ships, and that in action they would have acquitted themselves gallantly.

Lieutenant W. A. Kirk, U. S. N., who witnessed the surrender from a point of vantage on the bridge of the battleship *New York*, standing just behind Admiral Rodman and Admiral Sims, said that it was exceedingly difficult at the time to grasp the significance of their surrender and feel duly impressed, as there was a lack of show or emotion of any kind.

"The whole affair," he added, "was run exactly according to prearranged schedule, and was only another proof of the quiet, business-like, efficient way the Royal Navy does things." Continuing, he said:

"We proceeded into port in this formation, our lines gradually converging as we approached the entrance of the Firth of Forth. After reaching a point a short distance in the Firth the German ships dropped anchor, and Admiral Beatty on his flag-ship stood by to inspect them. As we passed within 500 yards of the enemy ships on our way to anchorage, we gave the British Admiral three rousing cheers. He returned them by waving his hat to Admiral Rodman. About three that afternoon Admiral Beatty sent his famous message, 'The German flag will be hauled down at sunset to-day, and will not be flown again until further orders.' The German ships a few days later, and after more inspection, were convoyed to their port of internment, Scapa Flow."

The American battleships remained with the Grand Fleet for about two weeks after the surrender, and then departed, amid many felicitations and interchange of compliments, to Portland, where they joined the vessels assembled to escort President Wilson into Brest. This done, the American sea-fighters lay for a day in Brest, and then, spreading 600-foot homeward-bound pennants to the breezes, the armada headed for the United States, where at the port of New York the men of the fleet paraded down Fifth Avenue, to the appreciative acclaim of tens upon tens of thousands of enthusiastic patriots who lined Fifth Avenue. . . .

Had the German fleet come out for battle a large percentage of it would unquestionably have been destroyed, and yet it is the theory of naval officers that some units, perhaps the swift cruisers, would in the very nature of the fighting (sea battles are fought upon the lines of two great arcs) have succeeded in shaking themselves loose, to the consequent detriment of our freight and transport traffic. Cruisers speeding free upon the face of the broad ocean are difficult to corner, and a great amount of damage might have been inflicted on the Allies before all were finally hunted down.

As it was, the enemy fleet remained at its base, and in the end came forth peacefully, as has been described. Had the war gone on, had the German craft not appeared for battle, a plan to smother their base through the medium of clouds of bombing airplanes would unquestionably have been put into effect at a good and proper time. And at the same juncture, no doubt, our Sixth Squadron would have joined with the Grand Fleet in an attack upon

WHY THE SUBMARINE FAILED 287

Heligoland, plans for which are still in existence.

In the waning months of the war it had become increasingly clear that the submarine as a weapon to decide the war was ineffective. Not only were the Allied destroyers and chasers armed with their depth-bombs, waging a successful fight against the undersea boats, but other methods were beginning to have their effect. Chief among these were our mine-laying exploits, by which, in October of 1918, was established a mine-barrage across the North Sea, which proved a tremendous handicap to the German U-boats.

Captain Reginald R. Belknap, U. S. N., commanding Mine Squadron I of the Atlantic Fleet, which operated in European waters, has compiled an interesting account of the important part played by the United States mine-laying squadron in planting mines in the North Sea. From the time the United States joined in the war, he says, our Navy Department urged strong measures, essentially offensive, to hem in the enemy bases, so that fewer submarines might get out, or, if already out, get back. A new American invention came to the notice of the Bureau of Ordnance, where its possibilities were quickly perceived. A few quiet but searching experiments developed it into a mine of more promising effectiveness than any ever used before, especially against submarines. This gave the United States Navy the definite means to offer an anti-submarine barrage, on the German coast or elsewhere, and the result was the northern mine-barrage in the North Sea, stretching from the Orkneys 230 miles to Norway, which the Secretary of the Navy's annual report characterizes as "the outstanding anti-submarine offensive product of of the year."

Manufacture of the mines in this country—they were of the non-sweepable variety—had been going on since December, 1917. The many parts were constructed by the thousands by numerous different contractors, who delivered them at Norfolk, where the mine spheres were charged with 300 pounds of TNT, and loaded into steamers, managed by the Naval Overseas Transport Service. It required twenty-four steamers, running constant-

SOWING OF THE GREAT MINE FIELD 289

ly, to keep the ten mine-planters supplied with mines. Only one fell a victim to a submarine.

Our mine squadron arrived at Inverness May 26, 1918, and twelve days later started on its first mine-planting "excursion." On this excursion, June 7, the squadron planted a mine field 47 miles long, containing 3,400 mines, in three hours and thirty-six minutes. One ship emptied herself of 675 mines without a single break, 1 mine every eleven and one-half seconds through more than two hours, the longest series ever planted anywhere.

On the seventh excursion, August 26, the commander of the mine force, Rear-Admiral Strauss, U. S. N., went out, and on the next, by the American and British squadrons together, he was in command of them both, on the *San Francisco*. The mine field on this occasion closed the western end of the barrier off the Orkneys, making it complete across. Of the ninth excursion Rear-Admiral Clinton-Baker, R. N., was in command. Altogether the American squadron made fifteen excursions, the British squadron eleven, and when the barrage was finished, at the end of October, 70,100 mines in all had been planted in it, of which 56,570 were American. The barrier stretched from off the northern Orkney Islands, 230 miles, to the coast of Norway, near Bergen. Its width averaged 25 miles, nowhere less than 15 miles —more than an hour's run for a submarine.

The barrage began to yield results early in July, and from time to time reports would come of submarines damaged or disappearing. It may never be known definitely how many actually did come to grief there, but the best information gives a probable ten before the middle of October, with a final total of seventeen or more. In addition the squadron should be credited with two submarines lost in the field of British mines laid by the U. S. S. *Baltimore*, off the Irish coast.

In summing up the work of the navy throughout the war one month after the armistice had been signed, Secretary Daniels paid the highest tribute to the widely recognized efficiency of Vice-Admiral Sims; he had also superlative praise for Rear-Admiral Rodman, who commanded our battleships attached to the Grand

EXTENT OF OUR NAVY IN EUROPE

Fleet; for Vice-Admiral Wilson, commanding our forces in French waters; for Rear-Admiral Niblack, our Mediterranean commander, Rear-Admiral Dunn in the Azores, and Rear-Admiral Strauss in charge of mining operations.

When the fighting ended our force in European waters comprised 338 vessels, with 75,000 men and officers, a force larger than the entire navy before the war. The navy, in its operations, covered the widest scope in its history; naval men served on nearly 2,000 craft that plied the waters—on submarines, and in aviation, while on land, marines and sailors helped to hold strategic points. The regiments of marines shared with the magnificent army their part of the hard-won victory; wonderfully trained gun-crews of sailors manned the monster 14-inch guns—which marked a new departure in land warfare—while naval officers and men in all parts of the world did their full part in the operations which mark the heroic year of accomplishment.

While the destroyers led in the anti-submarine warfare, the 406 submarine chasers, of which 335 were despatched abroad, should have credit for efficient aid, also the American submarines sent to foreign waters.

The transportation of 2,000,000 American troops 3,000 miles overseas, with the loss of only a few hundred lives, and without the loss of a single American troopship on the way to France, was an unparalleled achievement. From a small beginning this fleet expanded to 24 cruisers and 42 transports, manned by 3,000 officers and 41,000 men, these being augmented by 4 French men-of-war and 13 foreign merchant vessels, a grand total of 83 ships. In spite of the constant menace of submarines, only 3 of these troopships were lost—the *Antilles*, *Lincoln*, and *Covington*. All were sunk on the homeward voyage.

Four naval vessels were lost as a result of submarine activity—the destroyer *Jacob Jones*, the converted yacht *Alcedo*, the coast-guard cutter *Tampa*, sunk with all on board, and the cruiser *San Diego*, sunk in home waters by striking an enemy mine. The loss of the collier *Cyclops*, bound for South America, whose disappearance is one of the unsolved mysteries of the seas, will probably never be explained.

FOURTEEN-INCH NAVAL GUNS 293

The notable achievements in naval ordnance, especially the work of the 14-inch naval guns on railway mounts on the western front, which hurled shells far behind the German lines, have received adequate recognition from Allied authorities. These mounts were designed and completed in four months. The land battery of these naval guns was manned exclusively by bluejackets, under command of Rear-Admiral C. P. Plunkett, and work of the Bureau of Ordnance was conducted by Admiral Early, the chief of the bureau, one of our "ablest and fittest" officers.

CHAPTER XVII

LESSONS OF THE WAR—THE SUBMARINE NOT REALLY A SUBMARINE—FRENCH TERM FOR UNDERSEA FIGHTER—THE SUCCESS OF THE CONVOY AGAINST SUBMERSIBLES—U-BOATS NOT SUCCESSFUL AGAINST SURFACE FIGHTERS—THEIR SHORTCOMINGS—WHAT THE SUBMARINE NEEDS TO BE A VITAL FACTOR IN SEA POWER—THEIR SHOWING AGAINST CONVOYED CRAFT—RECORD OF OUR NAVY IN CONVOYING AND PROTECTING CONVOYS—SECRETARY DANIELS'S REPORT

NAVAL scientists learned much as a result of this war, but contrary to popular theory the events of the four and a half years strengthened belief in the battleship as the deciding element in sea power. The submarine was frightful, and did a vast amount of harm, but not so much as one might think. Against surface fighters it was not remarkably effective; indeed the war proved that the submarine's only good chance against a battleship or cruiser was to lurk along some lane which the big surface craft was known to be following, and strike her quickly in the dark. Within effective torpedo range a periscope, day or night, is visible to keen-eyed watchers, and all told not a dozen

LESSONS OF THE WAR

British and American sea fighters, of whatever class, were sunk as a result of submarine attack.

In the battle of Heligoland Bight early in the war, as a matter of fact, a squadron of British battleships passed right through a nest of submarines and were not harmed. The most spectacular submarine success, the sinking of the three fine cruisers, *Aboukir* and *Cressy* and *Hawke*, was the result of an attack delivered upon unsuspecting craft, which were lying at anchor, or at all events under deliberate headway. The American Navy, as already pointed out, lost the *Jacob Jones*, a destroyer, the coast cutter *Tampa*, and the *Alcedo*, together with one or two smaller craft, but that is all.

It will surprise many when the statement is made that, of all the Atlantic convoys, east or west bound, in the four years of the war, aggregating a gross tonnage of some eighty-odd millions, only 654,288 tons were lost through submarine attack, considerably less than 1 per cent of the total tonnage crossing the war zone during the war—0.83 per cent, to be exact. Here are some specific figures:

Atlantic convoys between July 26, 1917, and

October 15, 1918, a total of 1,027 convoys, comprising 14,968 ships east and west bound, were carried with a loss of 118 ships—0.79 of 1 per cent.

For all seas, 85,772 vessels, 433 lost—0.51 per cent.

It really boils down to the fact that the greatest feat of the submarine was in its success in *slowing up oversea freight traffic and in keeping neutral freighters in port*. In this respect the submarine most certainly was dangerously pernicious. But as a positive agency, as said, the undersea craft was not a decisive factor in the war.

All of which, most naturally, is a graphic commentary upon the inadequacy of the submarine as a check to the manifestations of sea power. In truth, there is a vast deal of popular misconception about the submarine, a name which is really a misnomer. The French are more precise in their term, a submersible; for, as a matter of fact, the submarine, or submersible, is in essence a surface craft which is able to descend beneath the water, proceeding thus for a limited time.

The amount of time which a submersible may

SUBMARINE NOT A SUBMARINE 297

run beneath the waves depends upon her speed. The best of the German undersea boats, it has been estimated, could not remain under more than three hours at high speed. They then had to come up, as the navy saying has it, for "more juice." To be more explicit, a submersible has a mechanical process, a combination motor and dynamo between the engine, which drives the boat when it is on the surface, and the thrust block through which the shaft runs to the propeller. This motor-dynamo, serving as a motor, drives the boat when she is beneath the water. When the electric power is exhausted the boat comes to the surface, the motor is disconnected from the shaft and is run as a dynamo generating power. Twelve hours are required in which to produce the amount of electricity required for use when the vessel next submerges. Thus, a great proportion of the time the submarine is a surface craft.

Again, there are important defects in the lead battery system, which was generally used in the war. First of all, they are very heavy, and secondly the sulphuric acid in the containers is liable to escape—in fact, does escape—when the boat rolls heavily. Sulphuric acid mingling with salt water in the bilges produces a chlorine gas, which, as every one knows, is most deadly. Not only this: the acid eats out the steel plates of a hull.

There is talk of using dry batteries, but these are heavy, too, and there are evils arising from their use which have made the lead batteries, objectionable though they may be, preferable in a great majority of cases. The British have a type of submersible propelled on the surface by steam.

The Peace Conference at this writing is talking of the advisability of eliminating the submarine as a weapon of war. Whether by the time this is read such action will have been taken, the fact remains that before the submarine could hope to approach in formidability the surface fighter, she will have to experience a development which at the present time has not been attained. The vital need seems to be a single propulsive agency for progress on the surface and when submerged.

An interesting table showing the success of the convoy system is herewith presented:

SUCCESS OF THE CONVOY

Convoy Atlantic convoys Homeward	No. of convoys	No. of merchant ships	Losses in convoy	P. C.
North Atlantic	306	5,416	40	0.74
Gibraltar	133	1,979	30	1.5
West African ports	105	944	6	0.64
Rio de Janeiro	22	307	1	0.32
Total	566	8,646	77	0.89
Outward				
Various sailings from British ports	508	7,110	45	0.63
Other Convoys				
Scandinavian (old system)	...	6,475	75	1.15
Scandinavian (new system)	...	3,923	16	0.41
French coal trade	...	37,221	53	0.14
Local Mediterranean	...	10,275	127	1.24
East Coast	...	12,122	40	0.33
Grand total	...	85,772	433	0.51

STATEMENT OF SHIPS IN ORGANIZED ATLANTIC CONVOYS
July 26, 1917–October 5, 1918

SHIPS

	Homeward bound	Outward bound	Total
Convoys	539	488	1,027
Ships convoyed	8,194	6,774	14,968
Casualties	74	44	118
Per cent of casualties	0.9	0.65	0.79

TONNAGES

	(GROSS DEADWEIGHT)		
	Homeward bound	Outward bound	Total
Convoyed	59,062,200	47,491,950	106,554,150
Lost	510,600	378,100	888,700
Per cent of losses	0.86	0.8	0.83
	(GROSS TONNAGE)		
Convoyed	43,196,740	33,860,491	77,057,231
Lost	364,842	289,446	654,288
Per cent of losses	0.84	0.85	0.85

NOTE.—The above figures and the casualties only refer to convoys which reached their destination on or before October 5, 1918, and do not include convoys en route at that date.

Fifteen cargo ships with a deadweight tonnage of 103,692, were lost during 1918 by the Naval Overseas Transportation Service. The removal of the ban of secrecy, vital during the war as a protection to vessels and their crews, discloses that 6 ships, aggregating 42,627 tons, were destroyed by enemy activity, 5 vessels, representing a tonnage of 44,071 tons, were sunk in collisions, and 4 vessels, totalling 16,994 tons, were destroyed by fire and explosion. Seventy-two ships were originally assigned to this service late in 1917, and when the armistice was signed, November 11, 1918, the cargo fleet numbered 453 vessels, including 106 ships ready to be taken over.

Crews of naval cargo ships faced many perils, including the menace of an unseen foe, the danger of collision, and the liability to death by accidents from inflammable cargoes.

Not only were these crews confronted with the normal perils of the sea, says the report, but they faced destruction from torpedo, collision, and other unforeseen accidents that might cause fire in inflammable cargoes. It took brave men to steam week in and week out

SUCCESS OF THE CONVOY

through submarine and mine infested waters at eight knots an hour in a ship loaded with several thousand tons of depth charges, TNT, or poison gas, not knowing what minute the entire vessel was going to be blown to matchwood.

It is on record that a convoy of fifty ships from New York was disintegrated by a violent storm in mid-Atlantic, and that only two of the number reached France under convoy. "Every ship for herself," the forty-eight others by luck, pluck, and constant vigil, all finally dropped their anchors in the protected harbors of their destination.

The value of a cargo ship is realized when it is known that under existing war conditions each ship cost to operate $100 every hour. Good, bad, and indifferent ships, old or new, fast or slow, were transformed into serviceable craft. The personnel of the Naval Overseas Transportation Service at the time of the armistice included 5,000 officers and 45,000 enlisted men.

The world has been so deeply occupied with figures and facts relating to the havoc by the

German submarine that little thought has been centred upon the work of the Allied submersibles. Yet in the way of accounting for warships one may fancy that they rivalled the Teutonic craft. Details may be given of the part which British submarines played during the war. This service destroyed 2 battleships, 2 armed cruisers, 2 light cruisers, 7 destroyers, 5 gunboats, 20 submarines, and 5 armed auxiliary vessels. In addition 3 battleships and 1 light cruiser were torpedoed, but reached port badly damaged. One Zeppelin also got back to port badly damaged after having been attacked by a submarine.

Other enemy craft destroyed by British submarines were 14 transports, 6 ammunition and supply ships, 2 store ships, 53 steamships, and 197 sailing ships. In no case was a merchant ship sunk at sight. Care was taken to see that the crews of all vessels got safely away.

In addition to carrying out their attacks on enemy war-craft, the submarines played an important part in convoy work. In the third year of the war one of the British submarine commanders carried out 24 cruises, totalling

22,000 miles, which probably constitutes a record for any submarine. In the first and second years of the war 7 British submarine commanders carried out a total of 120 cruises, extending for 350 days, all of which were actually spent in the enemy theatre.

Our submarines, too, acquitted themselves nobly on the other side, and when the story of the navy's activities is finally presented by Mr. Daniels, we shall have in our possession details not now to be printed. We may, however, say that battles, submarine against submarine, have not been unknown in the war zone; the fact that in addition to moving ahead or astern the submarine has also the power of dodging up and down complicated these fights in many interesting ways.

There has been, too, a great deal of misapprehension concerning the relative showing of the United States and Great Britain in conveying our soldiers to the theatre of war. At one time in the war, it is true, the British were carrying considerably more than half of our soldiers, but in the latter stages our transport service made gigantic strides, so that now the total of percentages is such as to enlist our pride. According to figures issued from the office of Admiral Gleaves, in charge of oversea transport for our navy, of the 2,079,880 American troops transported overseas, 46½ per cent were carried in *American ships, manned by Americans;* 48½ per cent in British vessels, and the small balance in French and Italian craft. Of the total strength of the naval escort guarding these convoys the *United States furnished 82¾ per cent*, Great Britain 14½ per cent, and France 2⅛ per cent.

Figures giving some idea of the records attained by convoys carrying our soldiers may now be presented, and they are immensely interesting. In the three months of July, August, and September of 1918, 7 American soldiers with equipment arrived every minute of the day and night in England or France. The banner month was July, when 317,000 American soldiers were safely landed. In September, 311,219 American troops, 4,000 American sailors, and 5,000 Canadians were successfully transported across the Atlantic. The largest single convoy of this month carried to France 31,108, and to

ACHIEVEMENT OF OUR NAVY 305

England 28,873. Of the troops transported in this month American vessels carried 121,547; British vessels 175,721, and French 13,951.

All in all, in patrol, in convoy duty, in actual combat, our navy in the war accomplished with utter precision a stupendous task, a task of multifarious phases—all performed in that cleancut, vigorous, courageous, painstaking, largeminded way which we, throughout all the years, have been proud to regard as typical of the American Navy.

SECRETARY DANIELS'S REPORT

SECRETARY DANIELS'S REPORT OF THE ACTIVITIES OF THE NAVY IN THE WAR[*]

The operations of our navy during the world war have covered the widest scope in its history. Our naval forces have operated in European waters from the Mediterranean to the White Sea. At Corfu, Gibraltar, along the French Bay of Biscay ports, at the English Channel ports, on the Irish Coast, in the North Sea, at Murmansk and Archangel our naval forces have been stationed and have done creditable work. Their performance will probably form the most interesting and exciting portion of the naval history of this war, and it is the duty which has been most eagerly sought by all of the personnel, but owing to the character of the operations which our navy has been called upon to take part in it has not been possible for all of our naval forces, much as they desired it, to engage in operations at the front, and a large part of our work has been conducted quietly, but none the less effectively, in other areas. This service, while not so brilliant, has still been necessary, and without it our forces at the front could not have carried on the successful campaign that they did.

Naval men have served on nearly 2,000 craft that plied the waters, on submarines, and in aviation, where men of

[*] Josephus Daniels, Secretary of the Navy, issued an official report on December 8, 1918, in which he presented the following full account of the work of the navy during the war.

vision and courage prevent surprise attacks and fight with new-found weapons. On the land, marines and sailors have helped to hold strategic points, regiments of marines have shared with the army their part of the hard-won victory, and a wonderfully trained gun crew of sailors has manned the monster 14-inch guns which marked a new departure in land warfare.

In diplomacy, in investigation at home and in all parts of the world by naval officers and civilian agents, in protecting plants and labor from spies and enemies, in promoting new industrial organizations and enlarging older ones to meet war needs, in stimulating production of needed naval craft—these are some of the outstanding operations which mark the heroic year of accomplishment.

Fighting Craft

The employment of the fighting craft of the navy may be summed up as follows:

1. Escorting troop and cargo convoys and other special vessels.

2. Carrying out offensive and defensive measures against enemy submarines in the Western Atlantic.

3. Assignment to duty and the despatch abroad of naval vessels for operations in the war zone in conjunction with the naval forces of our allies.

4. Assignment to duty and operation of naval vessels to increase the force in home waters. Despatch abroad of miscellaneous craft for the army.

5. Protection of these craft en route.

6. Protection of vessels engaged in coastwise trade.

7. Salvaging and assisting vessels in distress, whether from maritime causes or from the operations of the enemy.

SECRETARY DANIELS'S REPORT 311

8. Protection of oil supplies from the Gulf.

In order to carry out successfully and speedily all these duties large increases in personnel, in ships of all classes and in the instrumentalities needed for their production and service were demanded. Briefly, then, it may be stated that on the day war was declared the enlistment and enrollment of the navy numbered 65,777 men. On the day Germany signed the armistice it had increased to 497,030 men and women, for it became necessary to enroll capable and patriotic women as yeomen to meet the sudden expansion and enlarged duties imposed by war conditions. This expansion has been progressive. In 1912 there were 3,094 officers and 47,515 enlisted men; by July 1, 1916, the number had grown to 4,293 officers and 54,234 enlisted men, and again in that year to 68,700 in all. In granting the increase Congress authorized the President in his discretion to augment that force to 87,800. Immediately on the outbreak of the war the navy was recruited to that strength, but it was found that under the provisions of our laws there were not sufficient officers in the upper grades of the navy to do the war work. At the same time the lessons of the war showed it was impossible to have the combatant ships of the navy ready for instant war service unless the ships had their full personnel on board and that personnel was highly trained.

In addition to this permanent strength recourse was had to the development of the existing reserves and to the creation of a new force.

NAVAL VOLUNTEERS

Up to 1913 the only organization that made any pretense of training men for the navy was the Naval Militia, and that was under State control, with practically no Federal supervision. As the militia seemed to offer the only means of producing a trained reserve, steps were at once taken to put it on a sound basis, and on February 16, 1914, a real Naval Militia under Federal control was created, provision being made for its organization and training in peace, as well as its utilization in war. As with all organized militia, the Naval Militia, even with the law of 1914, could not, under the Constitution, be called into service as such except for limited duties, such as to repel invasion. It could not be used outside the territorial limits of the United States. It is evident, then, that with such restrictions militia could hardly meet the requirements of the navy in a foreign war, and to overcome this difficulty the "National Naval Volunteers" were created in August, 1916.

Under this act members of Naval Militia organizations were authorized to volunteer for "any emergency," of which emergency the President was to be the judge. Other laws included the same measure, provided for a reserve force, for the automatic increase of officer personnel in each corps to correspond with increases in enlisted men, and for the Naval Flying Corps, special engineering officers, and the Naval Dental and Dental Reserve Corps. It also provided for taking over the lighthouse and other departmental divisions by the navy in time of war. Briefly, then, on July 1, 1917, three months after the declaration of war, the number of officers had increased to 8,038—4,694 regulars, 3,344 reserves—and the number of enlisted men to 171,133—128,666 regulars, 32,379 reserves, 10,088 National Naval Volunteers. The increase since that time is as follows:

SECRETARY DANIELS'S REPORT

April 1, 1918	Officers	Men
Regular Navy		
Permanent...........................	5,441	198,224
Temporary............................	2,519	......
Reserves.............................	10,625	85,475
Total.............................	18,585	283,717
November 9, 1918		
Regular Navy		
Permanent...........................	5,656	206,684
Temporary............................	4,833	......
Reserves.............................	21,985	290,346
Total.............................	32,474	497,030

THE NAVY THAT FLIES

The expansion of aviation in the navy has been of gratifying proportions and effectiveness. On July 1, 1917, naval aviation was still in its infancy. At that time there were only 45 naval aviators. There were officers of the navy, Marine Corps, and Coast Guard who had been given special training in and were attached to aviation. There were approximately 200 student officers under training, and about 1,250 enlisted men attached to the Aviation Service. These enlisted men were assigned to the three naval air stations in this country then in commission. Pensacola, Fla., had about 1,000 men, Bay Shore, Long Island, N. Y., had about 100, and Squantum, Mass., which was abandoned in the fall of 1917, had about 150 men. On July 1, 1918, there were 823 naval aviators, approximately 2,052 student officers, and 400 ground officers attached to naval aviation. In addition, there were more than 7,300 trained mechanics, and more than 5,400 mechanics in training. The total enlisted and commissioned personnel at this time was about 30,000.

The Ships

On the day war was declared 197 ships were in commission. To-day there are 2,003. In addition to furnishing all these ships with trained officers and men, the duty of supplying crews and officers of the growing merchant marine was undertaken by the navy. There has not been a day when the demand for men for these ships has not been supplied—how fit they were all the world attests—and after manning the merchant ships there has not been a time when provision was not made for the constantly increasing number of ships taken over by the navy.

During the year the energy available for new construction was concentrated mainly upon vessels to deal with the submarine menace. Three hundred and fifty-five of the 110-foot wooden submarine chasers were completed during the year. Fifty of these were taken over by France and 50 more for France were ordered during the year and have been completed since July 1, 1918. Forty-two more were ordered about the end of the fiscal year, delivery to begin in November and be completed in January.

Extraordinary measures were taken with reference to destroyers. By the summer of 1917 destroyer orders had been placed which not only absorbed all available capacity for more than a year, but required a material expansion of existing facilities. There were under construction, or

SECRETARY DANIELS'S REPORT 315

on order, in round figures, 100 of the thirty-five-knot type.

During the year, including orders placed at navy yards, the following have been contracted for: Four battleships, 1 battle cruiser, 2 fuel ships, 1 transport, 1 gunboat, 1 ammunition ship, 223 destroyers, 58 submarines, 112 fabricated patrol vessels (including 12 for the Italian Government), 92 submarine chasers (including 50 for the French Government), 51 mine-sweepers, 25 seagoing tugs and 46 harbor tugs, besides a large number of lighters, barges, and other auxiliary harbor craft. In addition to this, contracts have been placed for 12 large fuel ships in conjunction with the Emergency Fleet Corporation.

Ships launched during the year and up to October 1, 1918, include 1 gunboat, 93 destroyers, 29 submarines, 26 mine-sweepers, 4 fabricated patrol vessels, and 2 seagoing tugs. It is noteworthy that in the first nine months of 1918 there were launched no less than 83 destroyers of 98,281 tons aggregate normal displacement, as compared with 62 destroyers of 58,285 tons during the entire nine years next preceding January 1, 1918.

There have been added to the navy during the fiscal year and including the three months up to October 1, 1918, 2 battleships, 36 destroyers, 28 submarines, 355 submarine chasers, 13 mine-sweepers and 2 seagoing tugs. There have also been added to the operating naval forces by purchase, charter, etc., many hundred vessels of commercial type, including all classes from former German transatlantic liners to harbor tugboats and motorboats for auxiliary purposes.

Last year the construction of capital ships and large vessels generally had been to some extent suspended. Work continued upon vessels which had already made material progress toward completion, but was practically suspended upon those which had just been begun, or whose keels had not yet been laid. The act of July 1, 1918, required work to be actually begun upon the remaining vessels of the three-year programme within a year. This has all been planned and no difficulty in complying with the requirements of the act and pushing rapidly the construction of the vessels in question is anticipated. Advantage has been taken of the delay to introduce into the designs of the vessels which had not been laid down numerous improvements based upon war experience.

Work Overseas

War was declared on April 6, 1917. On the 4th of May a division of destroyers was in European waters. By January 1, 1918, there were 113 United States naval ships across, and in October, 1918, the total had reached 338 ships of all classes. At the present time there are 5,000 officers and 70,000 enlisted men of the navy serving in Europe, this total being greater than the full strength of the navy when the United States entered the war. The destroyers upon their first arrival were based on Queenstown, which has been the base of the operations of these best fighters of the submarines during the war. Every facility possible was provided for the comfort and recreation of the officers and men engaged in this most rigorous service.

During July and August, 1918, 3,444,012 tons of shipping were escorted to and from France by American escort vessels; of the above amount 1,577,735 tons were escorted in and 1,864,677 tons were escorted out of French ports. Of the tonnage escorted into French ports during this

SECRETARY DANIELS'S REPORT

time only 16,988 tons, or .009 per cent, were lost through enemy action, and of the tonnage escorted out from French ports only 27,858, or .013 per cent, were lost through the same cause. During the same period, July and August of this year, 259,604 American troops were escorted to France by United States escort vessels without the loss of a single man through enemy action. The particulars in the above paragraph refer to United States naval forces operating in the war zone from French ports.

During the same time—July and August—destroyers based on British ports supplied 75 per cent of the escorts for 318 ships, totalling 2,752,908 tons, and including the escort of vessels carrying 137,283 United States troops. The destroyers on this duty were at sea an average of 67 per cent of the time, and were under way for a period of about 16,000 hours, steaming approximately an aggregate of 260,000 miles. There were no losses due to enemy action.

The history of the convoy operations in which our naval forces have taken part, due to which we have been able so successfully to transport such a large number of our military forces abroad, and so many supplies for the army, is a chapter in itself. It is probably our major operation in this war, and will in the future stand as a monument to both the army and the navy as the greatest and most difficult troop transporting effort which has ever been conducted across seas.

[The Secretary says the convoy system was "suggested by President Wilson." He continues:]

This entire force, under command of Rear-Admiral Albert Gleaves, whose ability and resource have been tested and established in this great service in co-operation with the destroyer flotilla operating abroad, has developed an anti-submarine convoy and escort system the results of which have surpassed even the most sanguine expectations.

Troops Carried Overseas

American and British ships have carried over 2,000,000 American troops overseas. The United States did not possess enough ships to carry over our troops as rapidly as they were ready to sail or as quickly as they were needed in France. Great Britain furnished, under contract with the War Department, many ships and safely transported many American troops, the numbers having increased greatly in the spring and summer. A few troops were carried over by other allied ships. The actual number transported in British ships was more than a million.

Up to November 1, 1918, of the total number of United States troops in Europe, 924,578 made passage in United States naval convoys under escort of United States cruisers and destroyers. Since November 1, 1917, there have been 289 sailings of naval transports from American ports. In these operations of the cruiser and transport force of the Atlantic fleet not one eastbound American transport has been torpedoed or damaged by the enemy and only three were sunk on the return voyage.

Our destroyers and patrol vessels, in addition to convoy duty, have waged an unceasing offensive warfare against the submarines. In spite of all this, our naval losses have been gratifyingly small. Only three American troopships—the *Antilles*, the *President Lincoln*, and the *Covington*—were sunk on the return voyage. Only three fighting ships have been lost as a result of enemy action—the patrol ship *Alcedo*, a converted yacht, sunk off the coast of France November 5, 1917; the torpedoboat destroyer *Jacob Jones*, sunk off the British coast December 6, 1917, and the cruiser *San Diego*, sunk near Fire Island, off the New York coast, on July 19, 1918, by striking a mine supposedly set adrift by a German submarine. The transport *Finland* and the destroyer *Cassin*, which were torpedoed, reached port and were soon repaired and placed back in service. The transport *Mount Vernon*, struck by a torpedo on September 5 last, proceeded to port under its own steam and was repaired.

The most serious loss of life due to enemy activity was the loss of the Coast Guard cutter *Tampa*, with all on board, in Bristol Channel, England, on the night of September 26, 1918. The *Tampa*, which was doing escort duty, had gone ahead of the convoy. Vessels following heard an explosion, but when they reached the vicinity there were only bits of floating wreckage to show where the ship had gone down. Not one of the 111 officers and men of her crew was rescued, and, though it is believed she was sunk by a torpedo from an enemy submarine, the exact manner in which the vessel met its fate may never be known.

OTHER POINTS SUMMARIZED

Secretary Daniels records many other achievements of ships and personnel, including those of the naval overseas transportation service. Of the latter he says in substance:

In ten months the transportation service grew from 10 ships to a fleet of 321 cargo-carrying ships, aggregating a deadweight tonnage of 2,800,000, and numerically equalling the combined Cunard, Hamburg-American, and North German Lloyd lines at the outbreak of the war. Of this number 227 ships were mainly in operation.

From the Emergency Fleet Corporation the navy has taken over for operation 94 new vessels, aggregating 700,000 deadweight tons. On March 21, 1918, by order of the President 101 Dutch merchant vessels were taken over by the Navy Department pending their allocation to the various vital trades of this country, and 26 of these vessels are now a part of the naval overseas fleet. This vast fleet of cargo vessels has been officered and manned through enrollment of the seagoing personnel of the American merchant marine, officers and men of the United States Navy, and the assignment after training of graduates of technical schools and training schools, developed by the navy since the United States entered the war.

There are required for the operation of this fleet at the present time 5,000 officers and 29,000 enlisted men, and adequate arrangements for future needs of personnel have been provided. The navy has risen to the exacting demands imposed upon it by the war, and it will certainly be a source of pride to the American people to know that within ten months of the time that this new force was created, in spite of the many obstacles in the way of its accomplishment, an American naval vessel, manned by an American naval crew, left an American port on the average of every five hours, carrying subsistence and equipment so vital to the American Expeditionary Force.

One of the agencies adopted during the war for more efficient naval administration is the organization and development of naval districts.

Secretary Daniels, in other passages of the foregoing report, declares that the record made abroad by the United States Navy, in co-operation with the navies of Great Britain, France, Italy, and Japan, is without precedent in allied warfare. He pays a high tribute to the efficiency of Admiral Sims, Commander-in-Chief of American naval forces in European waters; of Rear-Admiral Rodman, in command of the American battleships with the British fleet; of Vice-Admiral Wilson, in France; Rear-Admiral Niblack, in the Mediterranean; of Rear-Admiral Dunn, in the Azores; of Rear-Admiral Strauss, in charge of mining operations, and other officers in charge of various special activities.

The report tells of notable achievements in ordnance, especially the work of the 14-inch naval guns on railway mounts on the western front, which hurled shells far behind the German lines, these mounts being designed and completed in four months. The land battery of these naval guns was manned exclusively by bluejackets under command of Rear-Admiral C. P. Plunkett. The work of the Bureau of Ordnance is praised, and Admiral Earle, the Chief of the bureau, is declared "one of the ablest and fittest officers."

An account is given of the mine barrage in the North Sea, one of the outstanding anti-submarine offensive projects of the year, thus closing the North Sea, and for which 100,000 mines were manufactured and 85,000 shipped abroad. A special mine-loading plant, with a capacity of more than 1,000 mines a day, was established by the Navy Department.

A star shell was developed which, when fired in the vicinity of an enemy fleet, would light it up, make ships visible, and render them easy targets without disclosing the position of our own ships at night.

The Bureau of Ordnance, under the direction of Rear-Admiral Earle, is stated to have met and conquered the critical shortage of high explosives which threatened to prolong the time of preparation necessary for America to smash the German military forces; this was done by the invention of TNX, a high explosive, to take the place of TNT, the change being sufficient to increase the available supply of explosives in this country to some 30,000,000 pounds.

In the future, it is stated, American dreadnoughts and battle cruisers will be armed with 16-inch guns, making these the heaviest armed vessels in the world.

Depth-charges are stated to be the most effective anti-submarine weapons. American vessels were adequately armed with this new weapon.

A new type was developed and a new gun, known as the "Y" gun, was designed and built especially for firing depth-charges.

THE ACHIEVEMENTS OF THE MARINE CORPS

By Josephus Daniels
SECRETARY OF THE NAVY

The United States Marine Corps, the efficient fighting, building, and landing force of the navy, has won imperishable glory in the fulfilment of its latest duties upon the battlefields of France, where the marines, fighting for the time under General Pershing as a part of the victorious American Army, have written a story of valor and sacrifice that will live in the brightest annals of the war. With heroism that nothing could daunt, the Marine Corps played a vital role in stemming the German rush on Paris, and in later days aided in the beginning of the great offensive, the freeing of Rheims, and participated in the hard fighting in Champagne, which had as its object the throwing back of the Prussian armies in the vicinity of Cambrai and St. Quentin.

With only 8,000 men engaged in the fiercest battles, the Marine Corps casualties numbered 69 officers and 1,531 enlisted men dead and 78 officers and 2,435 enlisted men wounded seriously enough to be officially reported by cablegram, to which number should be added not a few whose wounds did not incapacitate them for further fighting. However, with a casualty list that numbers nearly half the original 8,000 men who entered battle, the official reports account for only 57 United States marines who have been captured by the enemy. This includes those who were wounded far in advance of their lines and who fell into the hands of Germans while unable to resist.

Memorial Day shall henceforth have a greater, deeper significance for America, for it was on that day, May 30, 1918, that our country really received its first call to battle—the battle in which American troops had the honor of stopping the German drive on Paris, throwing back the Prussian hordes in attack after attack, and beginning the retreat which lasted until imperial Germany was beaten to its knees and its emissaries appealing for an armistice under the flag of truce. And to the United States marines, fighting side by side with equally brave and equally courageous men in the American Army, to that faithful sea and land force of the navy, fell the honor of taking over the lines where the blow of the Prussian would strike the hardest, the line that was nearest Paris and where, should a breach occur, all would be lost.

The world knows to-day that the United States marines held that line; that they blocked the advance that was rolling on toward Paris at a rate of six or seven miles a day; that they met the attack in American fashion and with American heroism; that marines and soldiers of the American Army threw back the crack guard divisions of Germany, broke their advance, and then, attacking, drove them back in the beginning of a retreat that was not to end until the "cease firing" signal sounded for the end of the world's greatest war.

Advancing to Battle

Having reached their destination early on the morning of June 2, they disembarked, stiff and tired after a jour-

SECRETARY DANIELS'S REPORT 325

ney of more than seventy-two miles, but as they formed their lines and marched onward in the direction of the line they were to hold they were determined and cheerful. That evening the first field message from the 4th Brigade to Major-General Omar Bundy, commanding the 2d Division, went forward:

Second Battalion, 6th Marines, in line from Le Thiolet through Clarembauts Woods to Triangle to Lucy. Instructed to hold line. First Battalion, 6th Marines, going into line from Lucy through Hill 142. Third Battalion in support at La Voie du Chatel, which is also the post command of the 6th Marines. Sixth Machine Gun Battalion distributed at line.

Meanwhile the 5th Regiment was moving into line, machine guns were advancing, and the artillery taking its position. That night the men and officers of the marines slept in the open, many of them in a field that was green with unharvested wheat, awaiting the time when they should be summoned to battle. The next day at 5 o'clock, the afternoon of June 2, began the battle of Château-Thierry, with the Americans holding the line against the most vicious wedge of the German advance.

Battle of Château-Thierry

The advance of the Germans was across a wheat field, driving at Hill 165 and advancing in smooth columns. The United States marines, trained to keen observation upon the rifle range, nearly every one of them wearing a marksman's medal or, better, that of the sharpshooter or expert rifleman, did not wait for those gray-clad hordes to advance nearer.

Calmly they set their sights and aimed with the same

precision that they had shown upon the rifle ranges at
Paris Island, Mare Island, and Quantico. Incessantly
their rifles cracked, and with their fire came the support
of the artillery. The machine-gun fire, incessant also,
began to make its inroads upon the advancing forces.
Closer and closer the shrapnel burst to its targets. Caught
in a seething wave of machine-gun fire, of scattering shrapnel, of accurate rifle fire, the Germans found themselves
in a position in which further advance could only mean
absolute suicide. The lines hesitated. They stopped.
They broke for cover, while the marines raked the woods
and ravines in which they had taken refuge with machine-gun and rifle to prevent their making another attempt to
advance by infiltrating through.

Above, a French airplane was checking up on the artillery fire. Surprised by the fact that men should deliberately set their sights, adjust their range, and then fire deliberately at an advancing foe, each man picking his
target, instead of firing merely in the direction of the
enemy, the aviator signalled below: "Bravo!" In the
rear that word was echoed again and again. The German drive on Paris had been stopped.

In Belleau Wood

For the next few days the fighting took on the character
of pushing forth outposts and determining the strength
of the enemy. Now, the fighting had changed. The
Germans, mystified that they should have run against
a stone wall of defense just when they believed that their
advance would be easiest, had halted, amazed; then prepared to defend the positions they had won with all the
stubbornness possible. In the black recesses of Belleau

SECRETARY DANIELS'S REPORT

Wood the Germans had established nest after nest of machine guns. There in the jungle of matted underbrush, of vines, of heavy foliage, they had placed themselves in positions they believed impregnable. And this meant that unless they could be routed, unless they could be thrown back, the breaking of the attack of June 2 would mean nothing. There would come another drive and another. The battle of Château-Thierry was therefore not won and could not be won until Belleau Wood had been cleared of the enemy.

It was June 6 that the attack of the American troops began against that wood and its adjacent surroundings, with the wood itself and the towns of Torcy and Bouresches forming the objectives. At 5 o'clock the attack came, and there began the tremendous sacrifices which the Marine Corps gladly suffered that the German fighters might be thrown back.

Fought in American Fashion

The marines fought strictly according to American methods—a rush, a halt, a rush again, in four-wave formation, the rear waves taking over the work of those who had fallen before them, passing over the bodies of their dead comrades and plunging ahead, until they, too, should be torn to bits. But behind those waves were more waves, and the attack went on.

"Men fell like flies," the expression is that of an officer writing from the field. Companies that had entered the battle 250 strong dwindled to 50 and 60, with a Sergeant in command; but the attack did not falter. At 9.45 o'clock that night Bouresches was taken by Lieutenant James F. Robertson and twenty-odd men of his platoon;

these soon were joined by two reinforcing platoons. Then came the enemy counter-attacks, but the marines held.

In Belleau Wood the fighting had been literally from tree to tree, stronghold to stronghold; and it was a fight which must last for weeks before its accomplishment in victory. Belleau Wood was a jungle, its every rocky formation containing a German machine-gun nest, almost impossible to reach by artillery or grenade fire. There was only one way to wipe out these nests—by the bayonet. And by this method were they wiped out, for United States marines, bare-chested, shouting their battle-cry of "E-e-e-e-e y-a-a-h-h-h yip!" charged straight into the murderous fire from those guns, and won!

Out of the number that charged, in more than one instance, only one would reach the stronghold. There, with his bayonet as his only weapon, he would either kill or capture the defenders of the nest, and then swinging the gun about in its position, turn it against the remaining German positions in the forest. Such was the character of the fighting in Belleau Wood; fighting which continued until July 6, when after a short relief the invincible Americans finally were taken back to the rest billet for recuperation.

Held the Line for Days

In all the history of the Marine Corps there is no such battle as that one in Belleau Wood. Fighting day and night without relief, without sleep, often without water, and for days without hot rations, the marines met and defeated the best divisions that Germany could throw into the line.

The heroism and doggedness of that battle are un-

SECRETARY DANIELS'S REPORT

paralleled. Time after time officers seeing their lines cut to pieces, seeing their men so dog-tired that they even fell asleep under shellfire, hearing their wounded calling for the water they were unable to supply, seeing men fight on after they had been wounded and until they dropped unconscious; time after time officers seeing these things, believing that the very limit of human endurance had been reached, would send back messages to their post command that their men were exhausted. But in answer to this would come the word that the line must hold, and, if possible, those lines must attack. And the lines obeyed. Without water, without food, without rest, they went forward—and forward every time to victory. Companies had been so torn and lacerated by losses that they were hardly platoons, but they held their lines and advanced them. In more than one case companies lost every officer, leaving a Sergeant and sometimes a Corporal to command, and the advance continued.

After thirteen days in this inferno of fire a captured German officer told with his dying breath of a fresh division of Germans that was about to be thrown into the battle to attempt to wrest from the marines that part of the wood they had gained. The marines, who for days had been fighting only on their sheer nerve, who had been worn out from nights of sleeplessness, from lack of rations, from terrific shell and machine-gun fire, straightened their lines and prepared for the attack. It came— as the dying German officer had predicted.

At 2 o'clock on the morning of June 13 it was launched by the Germans along the whole front. Without regard for men, the enemy hurled his forces against Bouresches and the Bois de Belleau, and sought to win back what had been taken from Germany by the Americans. The orders were that these positions must be taken at all costs; that the utmost losses in men must be endured that the Bois de Belleau and Bouresches might fall again into German hands. But the depleted lines of the marines held; the men who had fought on their nerve alone for days once more showed the mettle of which they were made. With their backs to the trees and boulders of the Bois de Belleau, with their sole shelter the scattered ruins of Bouresches, the thinning lines of the marines repelled the attack and crashed back the new division which had sought to wrest the position from them.

And so it went. Day after day, night after night, while time after time messages like the following travelled to the post command:

Losses heavy. Difficult to get runners through. Some have never returned. Morale excellent, but troops about all in. Men exhausted.

Exhausted, but holding on. And they continued to hold on in spite of every difficulty. Advancing their lines slowly day by day, the marines finally prepared their positions to such an extent that the last rush for the possession of the wood could be made. Then, on June 24, following a tremendous barrage, the struggle began.

The barrage literally tore the woods to pieces, but even its immensity could not wipe out all the nests that remained, the emplacements that were behind almost every clump of bushes, every jagged, rough group of boulders. But those that remained were wiped out by the American method of the rush and the bayonet, and in the days that followed every foot of Belleau Wood was cleared of the enemy and held by the frayed lines of the Americans.

It was, therefore, with the feeling of work well done that the depleted lines of the marines were relieved in

SECRETARY DANIELS'S REPORT 331

July, that they might be filled with replacements and made ready for a grand offensive in the vicinity of Soissons, July 18. And in recognition of their sacrifice and bravery this praise was forthcoming from the French:

ARMY HEADQUARTERS, June 30, 1918.

In view of the brilliant conduct of the Fourth Brigade of the Second United States Division, which in a spirited fight took Bouresches and the important strong point of Bois de Belleau, stubbornly defended by a large enemy force, the General commanding the Sixth Army orders that henceforth, in all official papers, the Bois de Belleau shall be named "Bois de la Brigade de Marine."

DIVISION GENERAL DEGOUTTE,
Commanding Sixth Army.

On July 18 the marines were again called into action in the vicinity of Soissons, near Tigny and Vierzy. In the face of a murderous fire from concentrated machine guns, which contested every foot of their advance, the United States marines moved forward until the severity of their casualties necessitated that they dig in and hold the positions they had gained. Here, again, their valor called forth official praise.

Then came the battle for the St. Mihiel salient. On the night of September 11 the 2d Division took over a line running from Remenauville to Limey, and on the night of September 14 and the morning of September 15 attacked, with two days' objectives ahead of them. Overcoming the enemy resistance, they romped through to the Rupt de Mad, a small river, crossed it on stone bridges, occupied Thiaucourt, the first day's objective, scaled the heights just beyond it, pushed on to a line running from the Zammes-Joulney Ridges to the Binvaux Forest, and there rested, with the second day's objectives occupied by 2.50 o'clock of the first day. The casualties of the division were about 1,000, of which 134 were killed. Of these, about half were marines. The captures in which the marines participated were 80 German officers, 3,200 men, ninety-odd cannon, and vast stores.

But even further honors were to befall the fighting, landing, and building force, of which the navy is justly proud. In the early part of October it became necessary for the Allies to capture the bald, jagged ridge twenty miles due east of Rheims, known as Blanc Mont Ridge. Here the armies of Germany and the Allies had clashed more than once, and attempt after attempt had been made to wrest it from German hands. It was a keystone of the German defense, the fall of which would have a far-reaching effect upon the enemy armies. To the glory of the United States marines, let it be said that they were again a part of that splendid 2d Division which swept forward in the attack which freed Blanc Mont Ridge from German hands, pushed its way down the slopes, and occupied the level around just beyond, thus assuring a victory, the full import of which can best be judged by the order of General Lejeune, following the battle:

FRANCE, Oct. 11, 1918.

OFFICERS AND MEN OF THE 2D DIVISION:

It is beyond my power of expression to describe fitly my admiration for your heroism. You attacked magnificently and you seized Blanc Mont Ridge, the keystone of the arch constituting the enemy's main position. You advanced beyond the ridge, breaking the enemy's lines,

SECRETARY DANIELS'S REPORT 333

and you held the ground gained with a tenacity which is unsurpassed in the annals of war.

As a direct result of your victory, the German armies east and west of Rheims are in full retreat, and by drawing on yourselves several German divisions from other parts of the front you greatly assisted the victorious advance of the allied armies between Cambrai and St. Quentin.

Your heroism and the heroism of our comrades who died on the battlefield will live in history forever, and will be emulated by the young men of our country for generations to come.

To be able to say when this war is finished, "I belonged to the 2d Division; I fought with it at the battle of Blanc Mont Ridge," will be the highest honor that can come to any man.

JOHN A. LEJEUNE.
Major-General, United States Marine Corps, Commanding.

Thus it is that the United States marines have fulfilled the glorious traditions of their corps in this their latest duty as the "soldiers who go to sea." Their sharpshooting—and in one regiment 93 per cent of the men wear the medal of a marksman, a sharpshooter, or an expert rifleman—has amazed soldiers of European armies, accustomed merely to shooting in the general direction of the enemy. Under the fiercest fire they have calmly adjusted their sights, aimed for their man, and killed him, and in bayonet attacks their advance on machine-gun nests has been irresistible.

In the official citation lists more than one American marine is credited with taking an enemy machine-gun single-handed, bayoneting its crew, and then turning the gun against the foe. In one battle alone, that of Belleau Wood, the citation lists bear the names of fully 500 United States marines who so distinguished themselves in battle as to call forth the official commendation of their superior officers.

More than faithful in every emergency, accepting hardships with admirable morale, proud of the honor of taking their place as shock troops for the American legions, they have fulfilled every glorious tradition of their corps, and they have given to the world a list of heroes whose names will go down to all history.

To Secretary Daniels's narrative may be added a brief account of the terms in which the French official journal cited the 4th American Brigade under Brigadier-General Harbord on December 8.

The brigade comprised the 5th Regiment of marines, under Colonel (now Brigadier-General) Wendel C. Veille; the 6th marines, under Colonel (now Brigadier-General) Albertus A. Catlin, and the 6th Machine Gun Battalion, under Major Edward B. Cole. The citation says the brigade, in full battle array, was thrown on a front which the enemy was attacking violently and at once proved itself a unit of the finest quality. It crushed the enemy attack on an important point of the position, and then undertook a series of offensive operations:

"During these operations, thanks to the brilliant courage, vigor, dash, and tenacity of its men, who refused to be disheartened by fatigue or losses; thanks to the activity and energy of the officers, and thanks to the personal action of Brigadier-General Harbord, the efforts of the brigade were crowned with success, realizing after twelve days of incessant struggle an important advance over the most difficult of terrain and the capture of two support points of the highest importance, Bouresches village and the fortified wood of Belleau."